T0005784

RILKE'S VENICE

Rilke's Venice

The City in Eleven Walks

by Birgit Haustedt

Translated by Stephen Brown

First published in English in 2008 by
Haus Publishing Ltd
4 Cinnamon Row
London SW11 3TW

This first paperback edition published in 2019

Originally published in German by Insel Verlag, Berlin, in 2006 under the title
Mit Rilke durch Venedig. Literarische Spaziergänge.

The moral right of the author has been asserted.

A CIP catalogue for this book is available from the British Library.

ISBN 978-1-90996-163-0
eISBN 978-1-90996-164-7

Typeset in Garamond by MacGuru Ltd

Printed in the United Kingdom by TJ International

All rights reserved

www.hauspublishing.com
@HausPublishing

Contents

Introduction

'HE HAD NO house, no address where you could look for him, no home, no permanent residence, no office. He was always travelling around the world and no one, not even he himself, knew in advance where he would turn next. [...] One only ever met him by chance. You would be standing in an Italian gallery and sense, without exactly knowing who it was, that someone was smiling at you, a gentle, friendly smile.'[1]

Rilke criss-crossed Europe; he visited Russia and sailed on the Nile; he was as much at ease in provincial Worpswede as in the cosmopolitan city of Paris or at a remote country seat in Bohemia. And over and over again, he went to Venice: St Mark's Square and the Lido, the Doge's Palace and the Grand Canal were his intimate friends. He visited the city ten times; the first was a weekend in March 1897, the last, in June and July 1920. He valued Venice above any other place in Italy. Cápri, it is true, inspired some of his most beautiful nature poems, but Florence he ignored once he had reached adulthood – in his poetry too – and Rome he rejected altogether, complaining of the pervasive 'lifeless and gloomy museum atmosphere' and preferring when he was in the city to read Kierkegaard in Danish.[2] Venice, by contrast, enthralled and provoked him: 'For a long time I have been unable even to glance casually at a magazine or book without reading the word Venice; wherever I look, it appears before my eyes at the last moment.'[3]

Rilke didn't travel merely to recuperate, or as a hobby, or for a break from the everyday. Travel was a passion for him, a way of life – and work too, part of his profession as a poet. Rilke's travelling served a single purpose: he was always seeking impulses, stimuli, ideas for his writing. It was never an easy task. Rilke's poems did not come about just from sitting on St Mark's Square, sensing the atmosphere and then putting it on paper. 'Poems are not, as people think, feelings (one has those quickly enough), – they are practical experiences. For a single verse one must see many cities, people and things. [...] One must be able to think back to journeys in unfamiliar regions, [...] to days in quiet, subdued rooms and mornings by the sea, to the sea in general, seas, to night journeys rushing noisily by ...'4

Among the many places Rilke travelled to, Venice represented a special challenge, because no other European city has such a rich artistic tradition or so many artworks in so small a space – the city in its entirety is a synthesis of art forms. No other place is so 'loaded with literature', so often put into song or painting, verse or prose. For Rilke, finding his own relationship with Venice was the task of a lifetime. His engagement with the city was more intense than with any other except Paris: 'Because we are not finished with each other from one occasion to the next, and because we want to know what each of us desires from the other.'5 Venice was all the more challenging for Rilke because he neither wanted nor was able to rely on tradition. He went his own way, both in the city and as a writer: 'The point is to relearn from the beginning.'

His texts offer none of the conventional atmospheric images of *La Serenissima* as a city of decadence. Though his first approach to Venice was entirely conventional – he read Goethe's *Italian Journey* – he quickly laid it to one side, finding it too sober. And he criticised the Baedeker – the educated classes' favourite guidebook since the mid-nineteenth century – for its 'smug little stars'. That did not stop the young poet from exploiting the guidebook for literary purposes:

his first poems sound like the Baedeker put into verse. And although he was constantly complaining about his fellow travellers and about mass tourism, whose first growths he witnessed in Venice, he profited from the arrangements for tourists when he needed to. He booked his tickets and arranged his train connections in the Cook's travel office – which was comfortable and very cheap.

In 1907, on his first substantial visit to the city, he took a whole stack of valuable old books, which the Viennese Richard Beer-Hofmann had lent to him: he repaid the debt later, by dedicating his poem 'Venetian Morning' to his friend. In Duino Castle, not far from Venice along the Adriatic coast, he spent months in the castle's library reading everything about the city he could find, in Italian, French and German. In Venice he visited archives and libraries. Unsurprisingly, he read literary texts too: he even wanted to translate the sonnets of Gaspara Stampa, Venice's most important poet. And though that never happened, she found her way into Rilke's poetry in another way: in the first of the *Duino Elegies*, he refers to her by name.

He read the latest things as well. He got hold of Thomas Mann's novella *Death in Venice* in 1912, straight after publication. 'Masterfully direct' was his judgement on the first part. The second he found 'simply embarrassing'. (You may read the full quotation on walk number nine.)

For someone who declared himself to be 'almost without culture', Rilke was astonishingly well read. He was an energetic reader, but not a systematic one. 'Rilke's education was [...] the education of an enthusiast, eclectic and erratic, yet he absorbed and then distilled a subject with great clarity.'[6] As any enthusiast would, he shares his knowledge with us as well. His poem 'A Doge' (1907) for example, describes the art of Venetian politics in a nutshell – not in barren academic language, nor so that it can be taken in and understood at first glance, but distilled into poetry.

EVEN MORE THAN READING, Rilke loved to walk. He was a passionate walker. Stefan Zweig, who often went walking with him in Paris, went so far as to say that 'knowing every last corner and depth of a city was his passion, almost the only one I ever perceived in him.'[7] This was equally true in Venice. Rilke roamed the city for days on end, sometimes by gondola, but mostly on foot. 'My reading ended up being no use at all on this last visit [–] the best thing was that, with the help of my new topographical education, I for the first time grasped the whole breadth of the city, from San Alvise to San Pietro di Castello.'[8] In 1920, after many years of absence, the poet could still find any street he wanted in the tourist-free northeastern part of the city – and without getting lost, as he proudly declared. He was also proud that he knew 'an entity as incommensurable as Venice' so well that a visitor could 'ask him for any destination they wished in the labyrinth of the "calli" and receive the right answer.'[9]

Rilke often walked alone. On other occasions, Marie von Thurn und Taxis-Hohenlohe, his hostess in Venice, accompanied him. She had come to know him in Paris in 1909, through a mutual friend, the philosopher and essayist Rudolf Kassner (incidentally, one of Rilke's few male friends). The princess liked him immediately, though she had imagined him quite differently, 'not this very young man, who looked almost like a child; at first glance he appeared very ugly, but very likeable at the same time.'[10] She made up a new name for him, 'Dottor Serafico'. He, always respectful, called her 'dear princess'. For over ten years, she was the most important person in his life, a motherly friend, a generous patron and a warm hostess both at her castle in Duino and in Venice. Rilke stayed most of the time in her 'authentic Venetian mezzanine' on the Grand Canal.

A Venetian by birth, Marie was from the oldest nobility, and one of Austria's richest women. Greatly interested in music, painting and literature, she even collaborated with Rilke on translating Dante. The princess loved to put together sociable gatherings of artists and scholars. Her castle at Duino was the centre of Europe's cultural elite. Before the First World War, you could have met everyone there, from the Italian superstar Eleonora Duse to the Berlin curator Wilhelm von Bode, and the entire high aristocracy of Europe as well, including the princess's husband. Marie von Thurn und Taxis was a genuine lady: educated, generous and shrewd. She helped Rilke whenever she could. When he had trouble with women, for example (which happened fairly often), she supplied him with the most appropriate and clearest words.

Together the princess and the poet visited churches, art exhibitions and cafés. A typical Venice day might run as follows: after a 'little breakfast in an authentic Venetian locale, in "Fenice", a visit to the "Frari Church", or the Querini-Stampalia art collection, or the enchanting 'Garden of Eden' on La Giudecca. From there, a detour 'to an antiquarian bookseller, who showed us some items; as improbably gorgeous as the flowers; Rilke had a great fondness for beautiful materials.'[11]

When he wanted to get in somewhere, the poet spared no effort: he mobilised his connections, wrote letters and waited tenaciously.

Rilke paid attention to everything on his walks; the least conspicuous things did not escape him. He was unable to walk past a gravestone without happily reading it out loud. Sometimes he recited his own poems – only in 'worthy locations', naturally. He carried his notebook with him on all his journeys, 'in the pocket of his black satin waistcoat, buttoned up to the neck – for a time, the only eccentricity he allowed himself.'[12]

THE POET was particularly fond of Venetian painters' delicate portraits of the Madonna. Exploring Venice with Rilke means looking at pictures as well – all the time and everywhere. 'Because if Venice is in every object, every perspective, every reflection, then it is a thousand times over in its pictures: the essence of the city is in its pictures.'[13] Rilke knew every museum, gallery and private collection in Venice; he regularly visited the Biennale of the time. He didn't care about admiring masterpieces, the history of styles, or putting work into periods – the typical business of art history. Everything had to touch him personally, by suggesting a poem, for example, as did a painting by Carpaccio in the Museo Correr, or a picture by Tintoretto in the remote Madonna dell'Orto Church, 'The Presentation of Mary in the Temple', which inspired his poem of the same name. Linking the two offers a double advantage: his poem helps us to understand Tintoretto's painting, its use of colour, the construction of the image and its composition as a whole. At the same time, we gain a rare insight into the workings of Rilke's poetry.

FOR THE PRINCESS, her excursions, journeys and walks with Rilke were exceptional experiences: 'I've never enjoyed a journey more than when I've had the good fortune to be travelling with Rilke. It was not just that he saw and noted everything; he also absorbed everything in a different way, differently from normal people. It almost took your breath away. It was impossible to know what was more remarkable about him: the parade of objects, or the "glass that shows us many more" forcing a way into his inner self.'[14] The poet also liked to remember their trips together – in his own way. In the first 'Duino Elegy' he writes: 'Or else an inscription sublimely imposed itself on you, / as, lately, the tablet in Santa Maria Formosa.'

'Lately' was 3 April 1911. According to the princess's diary, it was a beautiful morning. She noted down a great many other experiences that don't come out in the poetry. How Rilke used to enjoy watching women, for example: 'The sight of her thrilled him, though one came across such noble physiognomies often enough in the Friulian countryside. "For goodness' sake, Serafico," I said, "don't start thinking you're going to save this woman as well." He had to laugh heartily.'[15]

When he spent time in Venice, Rilke almost always stayed in the princess's comfortable apartment on the Grand Canal. How he lived there, how he made himself at home in the aristocratic household, how he got on with the maid Gigia, we learn from Rilke's correspondence with the princess. Rilke reported everything to her: his swimming at the Lido before an evening at Duchess Mocenigo's literary salon, the most glamorous in Venice, his writing crises, the Scirocco, and his difficult relationship with Eleonora Duse. It was through the princess that Rilke first gained access to the highest circles of Venetian aristocracy.

Even when he wasn't staying at the princess's, Rilke loved the expensive, high-class life. Most of the time, though it punished his wallet, he stayed in one of the luxury hotels on the Grand Canal. Even during his first stay in Venice in 1897, when he was still a student, he had superior accommodation. An American whom Rilke had come to know in Munich, Nathan Sulzberger, financed the trip and the young men stayed at the Britannia Hotel, in those days one of the three best places in the city, with a lift, central heating and a view of the Grand Canal.

When Rilke had no invitations and no money of his own, he was surprisingly practical. That was the situation in the autumn of 1907: he desperately wanted to go to Venice, but didn't have a penny. He asked everyone he knew in Paris for the cheapest rooms. In the end the Venetian art dealer Pietro Romanelli was able to give him a tip: his two sisters rented out rooms in their house on the Zattere – with special prices for poor poets. This was a stroke of luck in another way: it was here that he met Mimi Romanelli, the woman who for a long time preoccupied researchers as the 'unknown Venetian beloved'. A stroke of luck for poetry too: Rilke's most important Venice poems arose from his stay in November 1907, though he did not write them until months later, alone in Paris – because a loving woman only disturbed the process of composition.

RILKE IS REGARDED as the poet of the inner world. No one has created inner spaces like him, using only words, words – like those in the *Duino Elegies* for example – that resist being deciphered. The critics tell us that Rilke is the master at depicting internal landscapes with no external equivalents. Everything external is translated into the inner world of language. But Rilke does not ignore reality, at least not in his Venice poems. Reading them on the spot, you notice how much reality, how much knowledge of the place and its history, enters into his poems. Rilke was not a dreamer, wallowing in his own feelings. He was an exceptionally precise worker in language, who, as you can see in Venice, always 'earthed' the linguistic landscape of his poems, and who needed to incorporate points of reference from the real world: 'You may well imagine how much these environments have influenced me, different countries, which my long-suffering, indulgent destiny has allowed me to visit over and again, not merely as a tourist, but actually to live in, in the liveliest engagement with these countries' present and past.' [16]

Rilke was not interested only in his own subjectivity. He wanted always to penetrate to the essence of a city like Venice, behind the façades. His best-known poem on the city, 'Late Autumn in Venice', is not only concerned with the decadence of crumbling palaces (though it's about that too). It also focuses on an abandoned industrial area: the Arsenal, Venice's huge state-run shipyard, once the economic heart of the city. Without the Arsenal, without commerce, labour and craftsmanship, Rilke is saying, there would be no palaces and no art in Venice. He investigates the foundations of art and arrives at economics, an almost Brechtian approach, albeit wrapped in the poet's shimmering language.

Rilke's Venice poems lead to the historic and artistic centres of power: to Venice's magnificent state church Saint Mark's in the poem of the same name, or to the Doge's Palace (in 'A Doge'). But Rilke was interested in more than the mainstream, official history. He loved to walk the byways in Venice as well. In 1900 he became the first to describe a part of Venice that had not been part of the city's consciousness for centuries: the Ghetto. With Rilke's little story 'A Scene from the Ghetto in Venice' in your hand (see walk number five), you may discover this district's remarkable architecture and history.

When we speak of 'reality', we do not mean photographic reproduction or some kind of realism. Rilke was a poet. He took perceptions, history, myth, experience, what he had read and seen and heard, and transformed them into the precise language of his poetry. That was his art. Even in letters, like this one to his wife Clara, exactness of language was vital: '"Venise": this wondrous, faded name, which seems to be cracked through, and which survives, it seems, only by a miracle – is as strangely appropriate to the contemporary reality of that empire, as "Venezia" once was to the strong state, its energy and splendour... . "Venedig" meanwhile seems fussy and pedantic, fitting only for the brief, unhappy period of Austrian rule, a name for filing, written on numberless rolls of paper by spiteful bureaucrats, dismal and inky.'[17] A great feat – the way Rilke here unfolds Venice's eventful history without dates or dull historian's language – merely through the variations in its name.

Letters are rich sources on Rilke's Venice. For the poet, letters were always 'working materials': he rehearsed in his letters thoughts and formulations that he would use later in his poems. 'Work and letter are in this case like a skirt and its lining' wrote Rudolf Kassner once, 'except that the latter is made out of such costly material that it may very well occur to you to wear the skirt with the lining on the outside.'[18] This is especially true of Rilke's Venice correspondence: it contains many of his most beautiful, lucid and poetic passages.

Rilke's very first writing about Venice occurs in his letters. At the end of March 1897 he wrote to his friend from Munich, Nora Goudstikker: 'I shall see Venice, or rather – and I'm looking forward to this even more – I shall be permitted to tell you about Venice.'[19] Over many pages, he takes the young woman with him on one of his first excursions in the city – Rilke has rarely written so chaotically, and yet at the same time so spiritedly and directly. (Nora Goudstikker, incidentally, was one of Munich's first feminists and ran, together with her sister, the renowned Elvira photographic studio.)

Later letters are small works of art, such as those to his wife Clara in the autumn of 1907, with their descriptions unprecedented in the literature of Venice, as if painted by Cézanne. The poet tried out many of his formulations several times over on different addressees. Some of the letters illuminate his poems, such as the much-discussed letter to Baroness Sidonie Nádherni von Borutin, which reads like a prose version of 'Late Autumn in Venice'.

Even the letters Rilke wrote out of duty are useful. When Gisela von der Heydt asked for Rilke's advice for her honeymoon in Venice, he had so little enthusiasm that at first he repeatedly put off writing the letter. But Gisela's father Karl von der Heydt was Rilke's most important patron at the time, so in the end he sat himself down and composed her a sixteen-page letter (with notes!), though not without taking a sideswipe at the groom: 'I must really limit myself to a few modest hints (as I see them) and leave all the rest to the Baedeker. No: far better to leave it to your own mood and personal providence, which on this happy trip will lead you to everything; (unless your dear husband is unwilling to give up the reins: which wouldn't be a great hardship for you).'[20] We do not know whom Miss Gisela put her faith in, but she would certainly have seen and understood a great deal of Venice with Rilke as her guide. Many of his tips – such as where to get the most beautiful parting view of Venice – hold good to this day.

RILKE NEITHER CREATED a new myth of Venice nor perpetuated the old myth of decadence. In place of a compact, unified image of the city, he bequeathed us a modern one. In his scattered poems, letters, stories and cryptic references in the *Duino Elegies*, he reordered Venice into something new and more personal. In Rilke's work St Mark's and Carpaccio shove up against the Ghetto, Venice's rise as a sea power is as important as the period of its downfall, state affairs stand next to anonymous incidents, pictures of the Virgin next to everyday experiences.

Rilke mapped Venice anew, in his own way, not systematically, but as an aficionado. We do not have to share his passion for Madonnas and his distaste for traditional trattoria. But we can learn from Rilke and his attitude to travel. He once formulated it as follows: 'That is the terrible thing: in other countries, most people travel in a sensible way. They allow themselves to be guided by chance, to discover beautiful and unexpected things, and a wealth of happiness falls, rich and ripe, into their laps. In Italy they run blindly past a thousand subtle beauties on their way to the official tourist sights, which mostly disappoint, because, instead of achieving some kind of relationship with what they are looking at, they notice the gap between their own peevish haste and the gravely pedantic judgement of the art professor, reverentially recorded in the Baedeker. I would almost prefer that they bring back from Venice, as their number one, outstanding memory, the good cutlet they ate at the Bauer-Grünwald; at least then they would be bringing back a heartfelt pleasure, something living, personal, intimate.'[21]

Living, loving and writing on the Zattere and in Palazzo Valmarana

Zattere, Ponte Lungo 1471

When, on 19 November 1907, Rilke stood for the first time in front of Ponte Lungo 1471, the Zattere, he was exhausted from a night journey by train, and disappointed with his first impression of the city: 'It is much more difficult to admire Venice, because it feels cold; and in the first moment it has something of the desolate atmosphere of an unheated room where one had hoped to warm oneself up.'[22] Besides, the Pension Romanelli wasn't exactly in the best location. The modest little two-storey building, in those days painted blue, today a faded, terracotta brown, stood on the so-called Zattere, on the outside edge of the city, south of the Grand Canal. The Zattere was built in the sixteenth century as a quay and was the unloading area for wood, the most important construction material for ships. Hence the name: Zattere means rafts. This wide waterfront pavement runs for over a kilometre from the Dogana di Mare, formerly the maritime customs office, to the Stazione Marittima, the passenger port built in the nineteenth century. The Romanellis' building stands opposite the Stazione.

The two sisters Anna and Adelmina Romanelli rented out cheap rooms in their house – like many others on the Zattere, which the

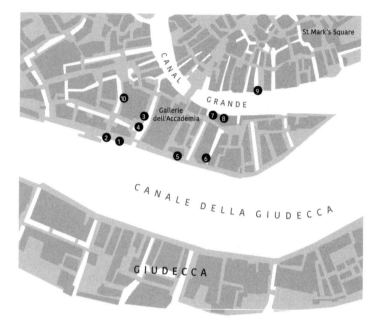

[1] **Pension Romanelli** [2] **the house where Luigi Nonos was born** [3]
Campo San Trovaso [4] **shipyard 'Squero di San Trovaso'** [5] **Church I
Gesuati** (Santa Maria del Rosario) [6] **Pension 'La Calcina'** [7] **Palazzo
Valmarana** (today: Cini-Valmarana) [8] **Campo San Vio** [9] **Palazzo Corner**
(Ca' Grande) [10] **Locanda Montin**

Baedeker recommended as good value and peaceful, though somewhat off the beaten track. Instead of the city centre with its art treasures, Rilke had landed up at the harbour: 'It's now night. The broad stone quay of the Zattere is outside. Large sailing ships lie along its entire length. It is so quiet that you can hear the ropes creaking on a boat further out. From time to time a solitary footstep comes and, though it has only just gone eight, it sounds late.'[23]

Pietro Romanelli, an acquaintance of Rilke's in Paris, had made the introduction and his sisters had invited him in a 'very nice letter' to come at any time. But when the poet arrived at their door, the Venetian women were astonished. On the basis of his second name they were expecting a young woman and now a man was standing in front of them, expecting to stay. Adelmina, the younger of the sisters, quickly recovered her composure and invited him in to have something to eat – a vegetarian meal in fact, which they had already agreed to supply, and for a very reasonable price. Rilke had the most beautiful room in the house, facing south, with a wonderful view over the Giudecca canal, which is at that point almost 300 metres across, and onto La Giudecca itself. Today the Zattere is one of Venice's loveliest places to walk and a favourite with the locals, especially in the evening and during the summer. A fresh breeze always blows, even in stiflingly hot weather, and it is almost like being at the seaside, though little of the atmosphere of the docks survives.

The pension was a stroke of luck for Rilke. He felt at ease immediately, and discovered Venice, as he enthused to his wife Clara, 'not from a hotel, but from a little home, with old things, two sisters and one maid.'[24] It sounds tranquil, unassuming – and boring. The house was old and the maid may have been as well, but at least one of the sisters was young, lively, and very beautiful: Adelmina, called Mimi. She took care of their guest from the start, playing the piano for him in the evening (she was an outstanding pianist, a pupil of Busoni), in the day accompanying him around a November Venice for hours at a time. By day two, she had given him a picture of herself. It was not without effect. The poet wrote her a letter in French: 'I experience your beauty like a child being told a beautiful story.'[25] A couple of days later he was already declaring his love to her – on his knees, in a gondola, as Signora Romanelli recalled it later. And the letters kept coming: 'My heart continues to watch you, kneeling. I love you.'[26]

The birthplace of Luigi Nono

Three houses to the left of number 1471 stands the house where the Venetian composer Luigi Nono (1924–1990) was born and died. Nono is the creator of an unusual Rilke composition. Unusual in the first place because modern composers have rarely set Rilke's poetry to music (Hindemith's *Das Marienleben* is the best known exception), but mostly because the work itself is unusual. *Das atmende Klarsein* [The Breathing Clearness] – the title is a quotation from the seventh Duino Elegy – could not really be described as a setting of Rilke's work. From 1980 to 1983 Nono worked closely with the Venetian philosopher Massimo Cacciari. This expert on Rilke (who could quote Rilke's Venetian poems in German off the cuff during a television interview) combined passages from the *Duino Elegies* with ancient Orphic poetry. Luigi Nono then set these words to music for choir and flute. The text is for the most part incomprehensible; the words fade away as if in the wind. One understands only scraps of text – similar to one's experience while reading the *Duino Elegies*. It is a congenial setting for Rilke's most difficult poetry. Massimo Cacciari, incidentally, later became the mayor of Venice.

Campo San Trovaso

A few steps back, past the Romanellis' house and around the corner, is the Campo San Trovaso. It looks the same as it did in Rilke's time.

Behind the Zattere used to be an area of workers and artisans. Fishermen, dockworkers and craftsmen, most of whom specialised in wood, worked here in warehouses, workshops and small boatyards. The eldest of these boatyards, the Squero di San Trovaso, which dates back to the seventeenth century, is located here and is actually still in business. All boatyards of this type lie on the water's edge, with wooden sheds for storing tools and working in the winter. In the summer, work takes place on the yard in front. It is a difficult and skilful craft: a gondola is built from 224 parts, made of at least eight different woods, always including oak, cherry and walnut. It takes eight years' study to become a master gondola builder and the secrets of gondola building are strictly guarded. There used to be hundreds of these *squeri* (the Venetian word for a boatyard). Today the Squero di San Trovaso is one of the last.

In 1920, when the gondola had already ceased to be the chief mode of transport in the city, Rilke described the result of all this craftsmanship in his inimitable way: 'Seven years ago, because the gondola was then still an affordable vehicle, one always sailed out along the canals into the lagoon, up against the darkening of the sky; one perhaps never entered so fully into the medium of the night, as when one was lying almost flat on the black leather cushions of this coaxing vessel, the only one that does not tear a hole in the night as it presses forward. However well you know the gondola, its consummate perfection always amazes; many of its particular features, its extraordinary length for example, seem the opposite of what is required and yet then prove themselves to be unerringly practical and insightful. How Venice brought forth this slim black ship from its innermost nature, a creation, an essence – in the world of objects, only a musical instrument compares to it, an object whose entire body is shaped by requirements that reach deep into the invisible and incomprehensible. Perhaps the gondola is silence's instrument, the gondolier stands there like a sign, like the treble clef, at the beginning of a line of movement, of noiseless, silent music, endlessly varying and intensifying.'[27]

SAN TROVASO is significant on a Rilke walk for another reason: Gaspara Stampa, Venice's most important female poet and one of Rilke's 'patron saints', died here in April 1554. The story of her life and love was a model for Rilke, because she became an artist as a result of an unhappy love affair. Born in Padua in 1523, she lived as a courtesan in Venice and fell in love with a count, Collatino di Collalto. He abandoned her after only a short time, but she continued to love him, hopelessly and despairingly, until she transformed her suffering into verse. She began to write letters and sonnets, so that her entire passion became art. She died aged 31. Rilke had a great soft spot for women who became artists out of unhappy love. He placed memorials to Gaspara Stampa in two of his major works. In his novel *The Notebooks of Malte Laurids Brigge* he glorifies her as one of the 'mighty lovers'.[28] In the *Duino Elegies*, Stampa becomes a kind of emblematic figure for the poet. One famous sequence in the first elegy runs thus:

> Does Gaspara Stampa
> mean enough to you yet, and that any girl, whose beloved
> has slipped away, might feel, from that far intenser
> example of loving: 'Could I but become like her!'?
> Ought not these oldest sufferings of ours to be yielding
> more fruit by now? Is it not time that, in loving,
> we freed ourselves from the loved one, and, quivering, endured:
> as the arrow endures the string, to become, in the gathering
> out-leap,
> something more than itself? For staying is nowhere. [29]

In his own life the poet interpreted the ideal of love without possession, as he called it, somewhat differently. In the case of Mimi Romanelli, for example. After ten days of love, passion and letters, he went away. She remained utterly in love with him for years; he soon distanced himself from her. By letter. Sometimes he played the good husband ('My wife is at one with me in admiration. We spend hours in front of your beautiful portrait.'[30]), sometimes he was too ill to visit her – he always found a pretext to avoid her passion: 'I beg all those who love me, to love my solitude as well,' he wrote to his former Venetian beloved, 'because otherwise I have to hide myself away from their eyes and hands, like a wild animal retreating from the enemies that pursue him.'[31] They continued to exchange letters for years. Rilke looked after Mimi as well: on one occasion he even arranged for Princess von Thurn und Taxis to buy a picture from her, when she was in great financial distress. But he preferred to keep everything at a distance. He only met her occasionally when he was in Venice, and more or less had to be forced to go walking with her. And he never wanted to stay with her again.

Rilke's ten days with Mimi Romanelli in November 1907 were his most productive in Venice. After his stay he wrote the poems 'San Marco', 'Late Autumn in Venice', 'A Doge' and 'Venetian Morning' – gems of the literature of the city. All, however, were written at a fitting distance from Venice and from Mimi, months later, in the spring and summer of 1908, on Cápri and in Paris.

Zattere, Ponte Calcina 775

Rilke's longest stay in Venice lasted from May to September of 1912. At first he again stayed on the Zattere, though a little to the east of the Romanelli house. As in November 1907, five years before, he had no money and was stuck in a big work crisis – now not in the middle of *Malte*, but having completed his great novel and the first two *Duino Elegies*. As before, he hoped the lagoon city would inspire him. Marie von Thurn und Taxis had offered him her apartment, but at first he refused, having enjoyed her hospitality for far too long at Duino Castle. Finding somewhere to stay proved difficult: 'My hope of finding something in a palazzo is receding by the day, the Americans have introduced a scale of prices that no one apart from them can match.'[32] In the end he again rented a cheap room on the Zattere, Ponte Calcina 775. He lived there from 9 May to 1 June 1912, with a landlord and lady 'who are very attentive to me' in a 'furnished room, of which only the view was convincing.'[33] To the princess he made the best of it: 'I may perhaps become very fond of my room, I live a great deal off the view, which, especially first thing in the morning, is beautifully composed and sweeping.'[34] The popular Hotel Calcina at this address today makes use in its marketing of the fact that Rilke wrote letters from it.

The Gesuati Church

When Rilke felt the walls of his small furnished room closing in on him, he sometimes escaped into the Gesuati Church, which is very nearby on the Zattere. This eighteenth-century church, built by the Dominicans, is most famous for its rich rococo interior. But it was not just the art that interested Rilke: 'I long for some kind of calm, I found a little by chance yesterday evening, the priest at the Gesuati told the story of Saint Andrea Corsini, the girls and women of my neighbourhood sat on the pews around me, or, you could say, I with them, – it was somehow all right.'[35] He sent the princess one of his rare picture postcards (Rilke hated postcards, preferring to use his own writing paper or luxurious hotel stationery). Text and image reflected Rilke's mood: the card shows a detail from Gianbattista Tiepolo's 1748 altarpiece of the Dominican patron saints, Catherine of Siena and Rose of Lima, holding the baby Jesus in their arms. Two women looking after a boy. Rilke's text ends: 'A thousand embraces. I am very unhappily miserably orphaned and uninspired.'[36]

Palazzo Valmarana

For a couple of weeks Rilke endured the simple lodgings he had chosen, but they soon grew hotter and more uncomfortable, and in the end he himself suggested to the princess that he should settle himself in her apartment after all: 'Princess, in June, if I am actually still staying here and it is possible to do so, perhaps I may move into your *mezzanino* for a couple of weeks and install myself in the huge bed *à la Tagliamento*; there I would be able to be truly at home, and it is cooler than my current room.'[37]

The princess readily agreed. In spite of Rilke's positive words, she had shrewdly believed his room was 'not very comfortable' from the beginning. 'Happy to be able to contribute something to his well-being, I hastened to put my small home at his disposal. It looked out onto a canal that flows into the Grand Canal, and gave one a magnificent view of Palazzo Corner and Santa Maria della Salute. [...] He very much enjoyed his authentic Venetian mezzanine: it was really very pretty and homely, even if a little cramped.'[38]

It doesn't take long to get to the Palazzo Valmarana (today the Palazzo Cini). Go three hundred metres along the Rio San Vio canal and you will see the magnificent palazzo. It is in the Dorsoduro, the same part of the city as the Zattere, but on the showy side, facing the Grand Canal. Here are many large, elegant palaces, which were popular places to stay in the nineteenth century for wealthy foreigners, particularly the English. Very nearby, by the Accademia Bridge, lies Venice's most famous museum, the Accademia gallery. It is a good landmark from which to find the Valmarana Palace. Rilke, who described the route to a number of visitors, André Gide amongst them, thought so at any rate: 'Palazzo Valmarana (not to be confused with the one of the same name on the Grand Canal) is called Palazzo Valmarana à San Vio and may be reached on foot from the Accademia Bridge. At the Accademia building walk past to the left and then turn into the first side street to the left. The last door on the left-hand side of the street before the 'Campo' (San Vio) is the entrance to Palazzo Valmarana.'[39] These directions still work. The main façade of the Renaissance building faces onto Campo San Vio, which is also the best place to look at the building.

The von Thurn und Taxis family did not own the palace: the princess had only rented a small apartment within it, her so-called mezzanine. Venetian palaces were generally home and office in one. In the centre was a high central entrance hall, the *portego*. Above it was the likewise very high *piano nobile*, with living spaces for the nobles and imposing reception rooms. At the sides of the building the storeys were subdivided to create more floors. These half-storeys or between-storeys are called *mezzanini* (from *mezzo* = half). They are built either between the ground floor and the first or right underneath the roof. In both cases, the rooms are much lower than the aristocratic space of the *piano nobile*. But, for Rilke, they had a special attraction: 'This is the charm of the Venetian *mezzanini*: nowhere else could low rooms be so large, so broad, so harmonious in their proportions (: because, as in life, so with interiors, spaciousness is in the end a question of proportion –) as if the rooms, out of their abundance, had imposed the restriction of being so low on themselves.'[40] The lower mezzanines generally housed workspaces, stockrooms, archives and offices, while domestic servants used to live under the roof. You can identify a mezzanine from outside by its smaller windows, whether square, rectangular, circular or oval. As the princess stated that both the Palazzo Corner on the opposite side of the Grand Canal and the Santa Maria della Salute Church on the same side were visible from her apartment, we can only be talking about an upper mezzanine: it would be impossible to see the Salute Church from a lower storey.

Rilke moved into the Palazzo on 1 June 1912, 'on Saturday, with my heart throbbing, a little like how it will be when one enters heaven'[41] – so beautifully could the poet say thank you. The princess herself records for us how the mezzanine was furnished: 'I had picked out every item of furniture myself. There was a quantity of watercolours, pastels and engravings, of the kind we both loved. A small library – perhaps sixty volumes of an "Antologia di letteratura italiana" from the end of the eighteenth century, bound in white leather – offered the poet enough reading that was both interesting and largely unknown to him.'[42]

When Rilke moved in, he made only a few changes, but decisive ones. First of all, a decorative initiative. The money he was saving on rent he spent on flowers: 'The *pendule* is going and the roses have already made themselves at home; I have installed hydrangeas on the little balcony of the entrance-hall and ivy, which hangs down from the ledge.'[43] He decorated the apartment itself as well: 'There were always only a few things around him, but flowers were always glowing in vases and bowls, perhaps given to him by women, perhaps his own affectionate purchases.'[44] There were roses in Venice for the whole summer 'in silver bowls, I never let them run out [...] – when no one else had any more roses (and they do become scarce in the Venetian summer), I still had them, as if they could not leave me.'[45] Most of the flowers came from the old garden of Princess Titi in Palazzo Bembo, one of Venice's most famous palaces.[46]

As well as decorating the apartment, Rilke rearranged the furniture. Though his changes were of a fundamental nature, he explained them to the princess in a manner as casual as it was elegant: 'I haven't moved anything, except that I have put the secretaire away in your bedroom, because it is too temporary for sustained writing, and I have made the corner by the two windows into my writing place.'[47]

He repeated this procedure on later visits. In 1920 he wrote, again from the Palazzo Valmarana: 'The princess has only a small, albeit very charming desk here, whose coquettish nature offers my writing arm no welcome or support. Gigia and I removed this wounded little item of furniture the moment I arrived.'[48] A decisive act: Rilke changed the attractive (but functionless) aristocratic dwelling into a place of work, his poet's workshop. Having disposed so elegantly of the princess's secretaire, he bought his own Louis-Seize table, stylish, yes, but secondhand: 'I have found a suitable old writing table in the Ghetto, which now stands in the place of your little secretaire, except turned to look out of the south-facing window, and the carpenter of the Casetta Rossa has built me an excellent standing desk, which doesn't disturb anything and, incidentally, is the most beautiful of all my European standing desks.'[49] In spite of the emollient phrasing ('doesn't disturb anything'), Rilke's claim is clear: I am working, in earnest. The workmanlike vocabulary underscores the implication.

Rilke never owned his own furniture and, though he designed, with Heinrich Vogeler, the furnishings for his marriage ceremony in Worpswede, he never had a bed, or a stove, or a wardrobe. He bought only what he needed to work: books, a writing table, and standing desks. His workplace was his centre, his shrine: 'There were always books gleaming on the walls,' wrote Stefan Zweig, 'beautifully bound or carefully wrapped in paper, because he loved books as if they were dumb animals. Pencils and pens lay on the writing table perfectly aligned, the sheets of unwritten paper were arranged into a rectangle; a Russian icon and a Catholic crucifix, which I believe had accompanied him on all his travels, gave his workplace something of a religious character, though its religiosity could not be linked to any specific dogma.'[50]

Rilke required something else in order to feel happy in his new chosen home: from the very beginning he sought to have a good relationship with his neighbours, the owners of the palace. They were of an ancient noble family: the mother, Countess Giustina Valmarana, and her daughter Agapia Arpalice, Contessina Pia for short, lived on the palazzo's *piano nobile*. Rilke was a guest almost every evening 'in the Valmaranas' high central room–, with the night outside the three arched doorways.'[51] Although Contessina Pia was, as the Princess remarked, 'very *en beauté*', Rilke, unusually, did not fall in love with her. He preferred another role: 'It was a summer in Venice (I am there often, one of the families lives there, an old Venetian one, in which I am allowed from time to time to be a little child of the house).'[52] A firm friendship developed, which lasted over a decade, with many little rituals. The Contessina always sent Rilke a calendar at year's end; Rilke supplied both ladies with reading and established one of what he called his 'book traditions': he gave them his own works and lent them books that he valued, such as a particularly beautiful edition of the sonnets of Gaspara Stampa. When in 1921 he decided to translate these poems, he asked Pia for their return. He repeated his request in 1923 and 1924, but did not get the book back – the only blemish on their relationship. Is this the reason that Rilke in the end never translated Gaspara Stampa's verse?

THERE WAS SOMETHING, however, to disturb this aristocratic idyll: the 'hellish' racket coming from the Campo San Vio outside the palace. Rilke's concentration was easily disturbed by noise. If the poet was right to be getting angry, it sounded like this: 'Dusk and night-time are grim experiences from the *mezzanino*, the old mischief, the noise of children on the square in front, grows over the course of the evening into a *déchirement* without equal, and lasts, at the end of a hot day, long into the night. In order to live quietly in Venice, one must have no "Campo" in the vicinity, for children gather en masse on every flat surface and in addition there are the bars, where the population try to imitate the children, all screaming at once.'[53] In a good mood, Rilke could fashion the din into dense, atmospheric, poetic miniatures like this one: 'And outside, the transparent sounds pulsate, the cries of birds, children's voices, fragments of song, which rise up suddenly and break off suddenly, a hammer striking iron, carpets being beaten, and the dry blows of brittle stockfish being hit against a marble mooring post. And in between, the handle on the fountain, steps over the Ponte San Vio –, no silence anywhere, *ever*, the very essence of noise.'[54]

RILKE'S STAY in the princess's mezzanine was his longest and most comfortable in Venice. It was just how he had always wished it: he was living comfortably, he had somewhere to work, and a kind of home. He lived there from 1 June to 11 September 1912, for a few days in 1914 and then for the last time from 22 June to 13 July 1920. He was well looked after by the housekeeper Gigia, who called him, with affectionate irony, 'quel poeta Maria', but did everything he asked. The Valmarana women nurtured him and the princess herself introduced him to Venetian society. So were these ideal conditions for making poetry? By no means. Rilke's artistic balance sheet for his Venetian summer of 1912 was a bitter one: 'Good, generous sanctuaries, as Duino was, and Venice straight after, have been no great help to me,' he wrote to Lou Andreas-Salomé. 'These specially crafted environments require in each case too much adjustment, by their nature they involve so many strange arrangements, and when you finally have got so far as feeling you belong, right then is the lie, that one belongs, complete. I was in Venice right through into the autumn, supported by dear, friendly relationships, but in reality I was remaining there from day to day and from week to week only because I did not know where else to go.'[55]

Rilke completed no major work in the beautiful home he had arranged so practically. In the crisis of writing and life that followed the completion of *The Notebooks of Malte Laurids Brigge* in 1910 the very best external conditions were useless. As a result, the poet wrote there some of his most poetic Venetian letters, which bring us closer to his daily life in Venice, to the city at the beginning of the last century, and to the artist himself.

But letters were not enough for him. A notable false memory of this period, in a letter of 1920, betrays his disappointment: 'I myself brought a few trifles, as chance would have it, during my lengthy stay here in 1913, – a couple of glasses, a small Italian library in uniform bindings from the *dix-huitième*, even the writing desk upon which I am writing to you.'[56] Everything is correct, except for the date (it was 1912) and the trifle of the library, which was not his gift to the princess, but belonged to her already. That Rilke should have believed he had given her the 'trifle' of at least sixty volumes, all in matching bindings, arose rather from his wish to bequeath to the princess a substantial and, more to the point, complete work – exactly that, in other words, which he was unable to supply his patron in Venice.

Antica Locanda Montin

Where to eat in Venice without being fobbed off with the usual tourist fare? Rilke agonised over this problem whenever he had to dine out. 'I made the stupid mistake,' he wrote to Marie von Thurn und Taxis in May 1912, 'of beginning by walking around a great deal, always among strangers, which has led to a kind of despair, and I cannot find anywhere where I may eat sensibly, vegetables are impossible everywhere and nearby tables affect my appetite and glut my ears with snatches of German.'[57] For Rilke, who could be unsettled for hours by 'sitting in a noisy local'[58] (as Stefan Zweig tells us), finding a suitable restaurant was doubly difficult, because he was a vegetarian: not an easy situation in Italy. He had been committed to this diet ever since he had met Lou Andreas-Salomé. During their first summer together in 1897, in Wolfratshausen near Munich, Rilke had, with Lou's encouragement, changed many things in his life: not just his forename – from René to Rainer – and his handwriting (Lou practised with him until his timid schoolboy hand became the writing of a cultivated artist), but his whole way of living. He wanted to live humbly and naturally, very much in line with the Lebensreform movement, which was then the fashion amongst artists and intellectuals. The most important element of the lifestyle was diet: Rilke ate no fish, meat only when there was no alternative, and drank no alcohol. He practised his vegetarianism rigorously. When, for example, he lived for a long time in Rome, he generally cooked 'oats, eggs, tinned vegetables and milk'[59] for himself. He had the tinned food sent over from a Lebensreform factory in Hanover.

As a guest at aristocratic houses, he irritated the servants with his for the time outlandish demands. The princess tells us of a visit to Duino Castle: 'Rilke wanted a strict vegetarian regime, expecting that a remarkable enhancement of his whole being would result. As he disdained to eat fish, I was afraid lest our provisions should be entirely insufficient. Miss Greenham was distraught.'[60] Rilke, however, was able to calm her: 'The cook was at first bewildered by my vegetarian diet, but now we are starting to accommodate each other a little. She is already on the mend and regaining her artistry. Today she was positively resourceful.'[61]

When he was alone in Venice, Rilke went 'often, following an old devotion, to the Grand Hotel for lunch, where it is quiet and relaxing and the menus are a little less robust than in the hearty little inns.'[62] When he was with the princess, however, he more often visited simple restaurants, as she seems to have preferred more down-to-earth places. One of these formerly simple trattoria still survives near the Palazzo Valmarana. The Antica Locanda Montin was then as now a favourite for its green pergola, under which one can sit in the summer. Gabriele D'Annunzio rhapsodised about this garden, Modigliani came here, Ezra Pound was a regular guest, Luigi Nono too. And Rilke?

On 23 June 1920, the day after he moved into the mezzanine, Rilke went there on his own: 'It's simply sad to sit alone on the long table at Montin's ...'[63] Whether he was missing the society of his motherly friend, whether he was pleased with the food or not, is sadly lost to history. Today Montin's is still a restaurant known for its artistic and intellectual clientele. It's not cheap and you had best book.

Through Venice's flood of pictures

The Accademia Gallery

The best starting point for looking at art with Rilke is the Accademia Gallery, the world-famous collection of Venetian painting. Rilke visited often: it was on his list of must-sees from his first trip to Venice in 1897. At that time he was studying art history, along with history and German language and literature, but his experience was the same as that of many other tourists, who race through the extensive collection of more than three hundred pictures. He just described it more elegantly: 'As with every art collection, little of significance from the Accademia remains in the bright light of memory.'[64] Rilke was passionately interested in art all his life, but not as a kind of bourgeois education. At university he was already incapable of following a predetermined, impersonal approach to art. He studied for six terms anyway, first in Prague, then in Munich, and then later in Berlin, and wanted to do a doctorate under Richard Muther, one of the most renowned art historians of the time. But he did not complete his studies: 'Universities have until now always given me so little; my emotions react so strongly against their manner. Though it is also the fault of my awkwardness, which never and nowhere understands how to accept anything [...].'[65]

Rilke abandoned his studies, but not his interest in art. On the

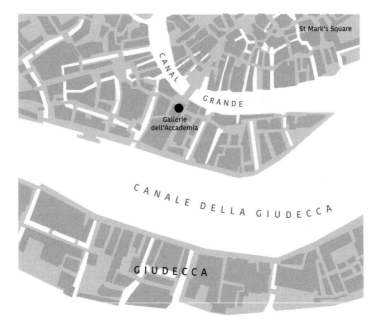

contrary. Few other writers have been so devoted to the visual arts. An ancient grave carving could inspire him as much as a Japanese woodcut, a Madonna by Bellini, a Picasso, or a sculpture by Rodin, whose biography he wrote. He was especially interested in contemporary art; he valued and admired the modernity of Cézanne, for example, before others did. He read all the art textbooks he came across, including the most recent, and was completely up to speed with the latest research. Rilke was an academically trained art lover with an unconventional eye. He wanted to 'learn to see', always afresh, without a grid or predetermined educational aim. His writings on paintings in Venice are more hints than detailed interpretations. You will come across no dates, artistic movements, or answers to questions such as 'whether this painting originates in the artist's late period or whether the "broad style of his master" asserts itself therein'.[66] Rilke offers us no systematic or detailed tour of the Accademia. He never made one himself: 'You know,' he once wrote to his wife Clara, 'how I always find the people who circulate around an exhibition so much more curious than the paintings.'[67]

Rilke was enthused by pictures that interested him personally and inspired his own art. On many occasions he wrote poems about paintings. In the Accademia you should, for example, look out for Titian's painting 'The Presentation of the Virgin at the Temple', which, together with a painting by Tintoretto on the same subject in the Madonna dell'Orto Church, inspired Rilke to write one of the poems in his 'The Life of Mary' cycle. (See walk number six.)

Rilke also offers a broad, very useful guiding thread through the many works in the museum. His key question of Venetian painting was: what does this picture tell us about Venice? Rilke calls our attention to the city's representation in art, in its use of colour, subjects, composition and overall effect. With Rilke, one 'reads' Venice's history in its pictures: galleries of paintings become like illustrated history books of the lagoon city. The poet assembled for Miss Gisela a vade-mecum through Venetian art. It begins with a kind of tour of the Accademia, which is useful still:

'To become an individual meant for each of these painters to become Venice. For them, being Venice meant: to have found oneself. The early paintings in the first room of the Accademia already demonstrate this truth. Later, it develops further and leads to Carpaccio (the Accademia and the San Giorgio degli Schiavoni Church); even the enigmatic dwindling flame deep within Giorgione (so he strikes me as a person) is more a development of Venice than a discrete personal vision. It is Tintoretto, however, who is the city's ultimate, its glory, its overflowing: the peak of Venice's self-confidence, awaking in painting, linking itself to all of history, grabbing hold of it and remaking it into Venetian history: all history, not excluding the Crucifixion (S. Cassiano Church), not excluding the presentation of Mary, which becomes a magnificent state occasion in the fresco in the Madonna dell'Orto Church, not excluding even the Last Judgement in the Doge's Palace. Only Titian arrives by the same route *beyond* Venice, at that unique, giant self, in which his great seniority has established him; but we have become so naively accustomed to seeing even in this towering figure only an aspect, an emanation of the essence of Venice, that the picture in which he has penetrated beyond the soul of the state into his own tragic soul (the stormy Annunciation in the S. Salvatore Church) would scarcely be attributed to him, had he (the ninety-eight-year-old) not written defiantly at its base "Titianus *fecit, fecit*" [Titian *made this, made this*] – twice.

'The painters who followed him, however, and especially those of the eighteenth century, can be assessed only in Venetian terms. Indeed, they are so very Venetian that these pictures by Tiepolo (in the Palazzo Labia among others), by Guardi (Museo Correr and the Pinacoteca Querini-Stampalia in the Palazzo of the same name, behind the beautiful Santa Maria Formosa Church) and by Longhi (in the same place) contain the entire secret of Venice. The secret as it revealed itself in their times, because it was in action, animated and exhausted by life.

'Thus these pictures (which have little importance as paintings, such as those in one room of the Palazzo Querini, which portray native lifts, games and customs) help us gain an informed insight into the essence of this world because they show it to us as a still living thing, which we must bring to life within ourselves in order to find and understand, behind its corruption, its reality and rules.

'Once one has seen a couple of Guardis and here and there a drawing or a small painting by one of the Longhis –: then will one climb into a gondola differently, relax inside it differently, and perhaps even, from time to time, deny oneself that pampered mode of transport, in order to get to know the strange small alleyways, which so unexpectedly deliver one onto a "campo" (only St Mark's Square is called a "piazza"), still without actually knowing how to continue on the other side, the easy verve of the little bridges which leap over the canals without a run-up, and the wonderful bridge-street of the Rialto, and the fish market, and the Erberia –, and the unexpected panoramas of open air, of expansiveness, of radiance, which over and over again present themselves to the walker –.'[68]

The Piazza, Saint Mark's, the Doge's Palace and a picture by Carpaccio in the Museo Correr

Piazza San Marco

Piazza San Marco is a square like no other. The Venetians think so: they don't allow any other square in their city to be called 'Piazza'. It is rare to be able to truly enjoy it, however, on account of 'the others' – the other tourists. They were already a problem in Rilke's day. In the face of this noisy irritation, even Rilke's beautiful words give up the ghost: 'The foreigners have overrun the place and, alas, if you cross over St Mark's Square in the evening you will find them all illuminated, lit up by the electric light; this stupid superlative of light banishes the last lineaments from their faces, they all look "Ah – Ah – Ah!"'[69]

Strangers and foreigners have always been part of the Venetian cityscape: at first businessmen and travelling merchants, then in the sixteenth and seventeenth centuries young noblemen, who began their Grand Tour of the courts of Europe in *La Serenissima*. From the mid-eighteenth century the well-heeled middle-classes came on their educational tours, and there were artists as well, in every corner of the city. The city was quick to profit from travellers; by the eighteenth century it was already developing a regular tourist industry. By the end of that century, in the last years of the Republic,

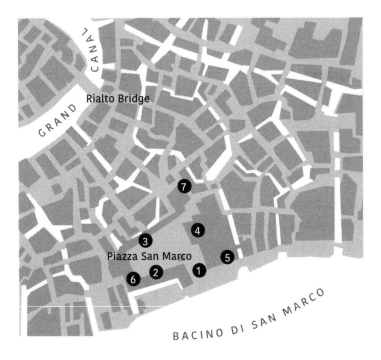

[1] **Piazetta San Marco** [2] **Caffè Florian Nouve** [3] **Gran Caffè Quadri** [4] **Basilica di San Marco** [5] **Palazzo Ducale** [6] **Museo Civico Correr** [7] **Spadaria**

the Venetians even concealed the death of the Doge for two weeks, so as not to endanger the tourist season in Carnival.

There was, however, a qualitative change around 1900. By then the tourists had become so numerous that they dominated the entire cityscape. Venice was the first stronghold of modern mass tourism in Europe. Having long ago lost its political and economic significance, *La Serenissima* relied on the tourist trade to ensure its survival as a front-rank European city. By the mid-nineteenth century vast hotels and beach facilities were being built on the Lido for fashionable swimming holidays and local public transport was being modernised – from 1883 steamboats, the vaporetti, were running along all important routes. By 1902 ten lines connected all the major locations in the city within five to ten minutes; the journey to the Lido took only twelve. The souvenir business was already by this time one of the city's strongest industries. In the high season tourists, many of them Germans, took over all the magical squares. Most of them were carrying the obligatory Baedeker, with its famous star system to tell them exactly what was worth seeing.

Even Rilke, on his first short trip to Venice in March 1897, travelled with the Baedeker, *Italy: Part One, Northern Italy*, the 14th edition, published in 1894. It was a practical book, the prototype of every modern travel guide, packed with information on everything from accommodation and where to eat (ratings included) to fares and the appropriate way to behave towards the locals (it offered, for example, advice on how to protect yourself against crooked gondolieri). Best of all were the suggested itineraries: 'On Sunday I must climb St Mark's Tower, storm the Doge's Palace and contemplate the Redentore Church, which interests me a great deal on account of Goethe having referred to it. There are enough churches in the city of beggars. But then I'll abandon my submissive attitude to the Baedecker [*sic*], and restrict myself to languidly marvelling like a local at the colourful hustle and bustle of the *canaletti*. I'd far rather wait somewhere in the heart of Venice for the first stars to appear at dusk over the high cupolas than lose myself in the little stars of the smug handbook.'[70]

Rilke cursed the other tourists and was irritated by them, but he considered St Mark's Square to be indispensable nonetheless: 'The Piazza – I think – the Piazzetta and, furthermore, the bright quay of the Riva, the Doge's Palace and the Dome next to it [...]: all of this, though it is at all times common property, can nonetheless be appreciated directly and unhindered, and grasped in its essence: it is so intense in its imperturbable existence, so vast, so solemn, of such grandly conceived effect, that everyone may have their own personal share in it.'[71]

Rilke himself often went to St Mark's Square, because Venetian 'society' met there, in Caffé Florian or in Quadri. 'Two hours ago on St Mark's Square I saw Mrs von Wallenburg, her brother and Pascha and accompanied them to Casetta Rossa; Prince Hohenlohe looked very fresh and seemed to me to be more animated than for a long time.'[72] Sometimes Rilke went to the Square precisely because there were so many people there: 'Most evenings I am on the Piazza, where one may have privacy in the general melee and I like to loiter over the spectacle of the moon above the lagoon and the quietly glinting façade of S Giorgio Maggiore.'[73] It wasn't quiet every evening, however, or at least only very late: from 20.30 to 22.30 on Sunday, Monday, Wednesday and Friday evenings there were regular concerts of military music.

St Mark's Basilica

'The craziest thing you can imagine. Varied in style and colour. – Mighty mosaics under broadly vaulted arches, like momentous eyes under serious brows. Above them, blithe, almost jaunty turrets, threatening capitals and resigned, aged cupolas. – The whole with a certain presumption and self-confidence. And the interior above all: an official reception hall for the Venetian God. – The entire church a courtly antechamber, with the real "salon" behind the elaborate rood screen. There the purple canons on comfortable choir stalls are in familiar, leisurely conversation with the fantastical Host. – The general public in the domed space half indifferent, half dozing, a few men praying, a few striking poses.'[74]

This passage comes from Rilke's first letter from Venice to Nora Goudstikker, on 28 March 1897, 'late at night on my first day of many faces'. A little muddled, but not bad for a first impression, this sketch of St Mark's Basilica. And yet no comparison to his poem 'San Marco' of ten years later:

San Marco
Venice
In this interior which, as excavated,
arches and twists within the golden foil,
round-cornered, glistening as with precious oil,
this city's darkness was accommodated

and secretly heaped up to balance out
that overplus of brightness, so pervading
all her possessions they were almost fading. –
And 'Aren't they fading?' comes the sudden doubt;

and, thrusting back the minish gallery
suspended near the vaulting's golden gleam,
you hail the unimpaired illumination

of that wide view; yet somehow mournfully
measuring its fatigued continuation
with that of the adjacent four-horse team.[75]

Here Rilke fits Stefan Zweig's description of him as a 'Master of words that seem wrought by the goldsmith's illustrious art.'[76] With this poem, Rilke proves himself a craftsman of language, in the best sense. The poem reproduces the richness of the church in the richness of its language. As the great Italy expert and travel writer, Eckart Peterich, has suggested, Rilke's poetry captures the architectural and aesthetic particularities of San Marco with unusual precision. It is no coincidence that this Christian church is reminiscent of an oriental place of worship: it was modelled on Hagia Sophia in Constantinople. Many of its stylistic features are Byzantine, but combined in a special way. Peterich's description of the church takes its lead from Rilke's: 'It is Byzantine most of all in its mosaic decorations, but also in the cavernous nature of the building, the rounding of every edge, the softness, the undulation, the passion for vaulting, the dissolution of every architectural form into painterly form: into golden light and glassy colours, as described in Rilke's poem:

In this interior which, as excavated,
arches and twists within the golden foil,
round-cornered, glistening as with precious oil,
this city's darkness was accommodated

and secretly heaped up

'The use of such a great diversity of building materials and forms contributes to this dissolution: all kinds of marble (more than three hundred), in every colour and grain, bloody porphyry, translucent alabaster, glistening granite, capitals from every period and in every style; bronze, brass and gemstones; marble and glass mosaic.'[77]

The church is a mix of styles and materials, but all this multiplicity has a unified basis. St Mark's was never merely a church. On the contrary, it had a single, pre-eminent aim: to demonstrate, beyond any doubt, the power of the state. To make it do so, the Venetians decorated the basilica with the most beautiful and expensive objects they had captured on their raiding expeditions: the whole church is a gigantic gathering of plunder from East and West. The most valuable and symbolically significant piece of booty also appears in Rilke's poem: the chariot with its 'four-horse team'. These are the oldest surviving ancient sculptures of horses, looted by the Venetians during their pillaging of Constantinople in 1204. The Venetians chose to install this valuable sculpture not among their government buildings, but in a church, triumphant in the middle of the façade, over the main entrance of St Mark's. The quadriga symbolises the most significant event in Venice's history: the victory over Byzantium and the founding of the city's Eastern empire.

You can admire the team of horses, which Napoleon at one point carried off to Paris, in replica form on the façade – the best view is from the terrace of the church. The original horses reside in the Basilica's museum.

You can see one section of the 4,000 square metres of mosaic, so scintillatingly described in Rilke's poem, close-up from the gallery. Rilke did so, or at any rate he gave Gisela von der Heydt the following tip: 'I would recommend that you climb up to the upper gallery in S. Marco' from where you may observe 'this mine' in which 'the vaults seem like the fractured surfaces of gold hauled from the earth.'[78] A good example of how Rilke tried out formulations for his poetry in a letter first. He wrote to Fräulein Gisela from Càpri on 24 March 1908. The poem 'San Marco' made its first appearance a few weeks later in Paris.

The Doge's Palace

'A wonderful interpretation of the façade of the Doge's Palace occurred to me recently: it represents the "mask of the state":

looked at in this way, the closeness of the windows to the grille-covered arcading of the two lower storeys, which fits with the points descending from the mask-face above, gains an uncannily telling significance, and even if a much later Venice has imposed this interpretation onto the older building, it would still always have been true to the attitude of the state, the anonymity of its rule.'[79] In Venice, the aesthetic was never an end in itself. In the Doge's Palace, the principles of *La Serenissima*'s government become architecture. How government *à la veneziana* functioned, what role the Doge played therein, what power the state had, and how it was manifest in architecture, can all be read in a poem by Rilke. 'A Doge' is not actually explicitly connected to a concrete location, but the implicit setting of the poem is the Doge's Palace.

A Doge

Ambassadors observed their intricateness
about him and his whole activity;
while they themselves were luring him to greatness,
they circumscribed the golden dogacy

with still more spies and limitations, ever
fearful that power might rend them limb from limb
which they were feeding (like a lion) in him
so circumspectly. He, though, never,

protected by his half-obscured sensation,
came to perceive this, and without cessation
kept growing greater. What the Council now

thought quelled within him by their practices,
he quelled himself. In that grey head of his
it was subdued. His countenance showed how.[80]

The assembled nobility of the city elected the Doge as head of state for life. He lived in the city's most magnificent palace, wore the most beautiful clothes, had everyone dancing attendance upon him. He lived in a 'golden dogacy', Rilke writes, an allusion to the famous Scala d'Oro, an imposing staircase decorated with gilded stucco reliefs, which leads up to the living quarters of the Palace on the second storey. But, as becomes apparent in Rilke's poem, the golden Dogeship was also a golden cage. The office was gilded, because in reality the Doge had no personal power. At his coronation he swore to carry out every instruction of the grand council and of other official bodies. Though the Doge chaired every council meeting, he really only signed things off: a kind of constitutional monarchy. Nominally, he was the state's most senior figure; in truth the Doge's power was pretty restricted. He could conduct no business transactions, nor accept any gifts, and no member of his family was allowed to hold public office. Over the course of the centuries more and more prohibitions were added. In the end, the Doge had to have his every letter approved.

In public the Doge still represented the power of the state, with all the elaborate splendour and trappings of power. In his poem Rilke uses a precise image for the situation: those around the Doge are feeding his power 'like a lion'. The lion was the symbol of the might of the Venetian state, and outwardly the Doge was this lion. But in actuality the Republic had control over him, like a lion in a cage. The entire government was built around the power of the state, not the individual ruler. It's no coincidence that there are hardly any prominent or well-known Doges. It's also no coincidence that Rilke, in spite of his penchant for resonant aristocratic names, gave his poem only the plain and anonymous title: 'A Doge'.

Rilke's poem highlights another peculiarity of the Venetian political system (and of the Doge's Palace). Rilke writes that the office of Doge is surrounded by 'spies and limitations'. This should be taken entirely literally: Venice had a sophisticated system of informers and the government's inquisitors were based in the Doge's Palace. On the one hand were the supremely luminous works of Tiepolo, Titian and Tintoretto; on the other, not far from the Doge's apartments and the magnificent government chambers, was a room, almost without light, draped in black. Anyone who ended up here, having been denounced by informers and 'spies', was doomed. Venice's secret police were renowned for their cruelty. The condemned did not have far to go, as the prison lay just next door to the Doge's Palace, separated only by the famous Bridge of Sighs: another example of a peculiarity of Venetian rule and Venetian architecture that you will learn to see through reading Rilke.

A picture by Carpaccio in the Museo Civico Correr

The Museo Civico Correr on St Mark's Square has one attraction for Rilke enthusiasts: alongside the model ships, old maps of the city, coins and flags there hangs here one of the most famous and puzzling pictures by the Venetian painter Vittorio Carpaccio, which inspired Rilke to write his poem 'The Courtesan'. This painting from the year 1495 shows two blonde ladies with rather weary, bored eyes and deep décolletages. They are sitting outside in front of a marble balustrade on a roof terrace or balcony. One of them is patting a small white dog.

> *The Courtesan*
> The sun of Venice in my hair's preparing
> a gold where lustrously shall culminate
> all alchemy. My brows, which emulate
> her bridges, you can contemplate
>
> over the silent perilousness repairing

of eyes which some communion secretly
unites with her canals, so that the sea
rises and ebbs and changes in them. He

who once has seen me falls to envying
my dog, because, in moments of distraction,
this hand no fieriness incinerates,

scathless, bejewelled, there recuperates. –
And many a hopeful youth of high extraction
will not survive my mouth's envenoming.[81]

The courtesan – another facet of the myth of Venice. The city
had been famous since the Renaissance for the skill of its courtesans
– their beauty, sensuality and venality. The courtesans were particularly admired for their blonde hair, which was in reality a kind of
strawberry blonde – and rarely natural. As Rilke writes: 'The sun of
Venice in my hair's preparing / a gold'. This is exactly right, in two
senses: in order to achieve this particular shade of hair colour, the
women sat out in the sun for hours on end on the *altana*, a charac-
teristically Venetian kind of terrace, generally of wood, built on the
roof and used, then and now, as a refuge from the sultry heat of the
Scirocco. The famous Venetian blonde was not a natural colour, but
an artefact, its golden tone the result of a complex and laborious
procedure. Thus the women used nature, the sun, a natural resource
which is available everywhere, to make gold – that is, money. Yellow
= gold = cash. Everything in Venice is turned into money – another
part of the Venice myth, as shown in Rilke's poem.

Prostitution had been an important sector of the Venetian
economy since the Renaissance, a legitimate source of profit for
nobles and businessmen. Venice made good money out of its prostitutes and fed its reputation as a city of carnality, courtesans and

love for sale. Rilke goes further: he represents the whole city as a courtesan, the courtesan becomes an allegory for the city, an eternal metamorphosis of the body of the city, linking it to female beauty, alchemy and money.

ps: In the 1950s art historians discovered that Carpaccio's painting does not in fact depict courtesans. Various clues, such as the crest of the Venetian patrician Torella family, which decorates the vase in the painting, suggest women of higher social status. Today the picture is called 'Two Venetian Ladies'. That even experts, however, should have confused aristocratic women with whores for so long is not so surprising, because the courtesans modelled themselves on upper-class women, dressed, spoke and wrote like them. And the ladies of Venetian 'high society' were not exactly virtuous either. Which is also represented: many of the details of Carpaccio's picture suggest an atmosphere of weary and highly refined sensuality. The women's flowing dresses in yellowy gold and crimson, with their pleats and expensively bejewelled décolletages contribute to the effect, as do the parrot and peacock, traditional painters' symbols of the erotic. Everything is highly cultivated; sexuality seems to have been completely subdued. But Rilke draws our attention to the many other layers in Carpaccio's picture. For example, the woman, who is the subject of Rilke's poem, fondles the small white dog with one hand, while with the other warding off a snarling pedigree dog. Though sensuality may have been domesticated, it is still dangerous. In Rilke's text, this is true of Venice too. The Venetians have tamed nature more than anyone else, they have forced the sea into canals, where it 'rises and ebbs and changes'. But nature's underlying threat to every culture and civilisation remains.

The Arsenal, Scuola Dalmata di San Giorgio degli Schiavoni, Campo Santa Maria Formosa and the Pinacoteca Querini-Stampalia

The Arsenal

Late Autumn in Venice

The city drifts no longer like a bait now,
upcatching all the days as they emerge.
Brittlier the glass palaces vibrate now
beneath your gaze. And from each garden verge

the summer like a bunch of puppets dangles,
headforemost, weary, made away.
Out of the ground, though, from dead forest tangles
volition mounts: as though before next daydreaming

the sea-commander must have rigged and ready
the galleys in the sleepless Arsenal,
and earliest morning air be tarred already

by an armada, oaringly outpressing,
and suddenly, with flare of flags, possessing
the great wind, radiant and invincible.[82]

[1] Museo Storico Navale [2] Scuola Dalmata di San Giorgio degli
Schiavoni [3] Pinacotecca Querini Stampalia [4] Campo Santa Maria
Formosa [5] Church Santa Maria Formosa

'Late Autumn in Venice', Rilke's best-known poem about the lagoon city, leads us away from its touristic and artistic centres. We end up not on the Grand Canal or St Mark's Square, but well to the east, at the Arsenal, what used to be the state shipyard. For Rilke, Venice's true centre was here: 'Think about it, it seems strange to me that people had the idea of exploiting this city for dreamy moods; she is perfect and forlorn, and so she allows it to happen. But if you walk through the alleyways echoing with the harsh sea wind, if you see the sharp edges of the water beating against the palaces, quite deliberately, rebelliously, triumphantly, and if you do not overlook the Arsenal beyond the splendour of the squares, the Arsenal, which has transformed forests into fleets, and the weight of the fleets into the wings of victory; if you reflect that the dearth of flowers gave birth to lace and that for lack of mines goods were made out of glass like gemstones, and that the entire world bought into this exquisite fraud and gave up their gold for it –, and that the space for the actual doing of all this didn't exist at all, that the city's land had itself first to be built of wood: then the scale of the deed, what has been brought together here, will terrify you, and you will feel its presence ever after, challenging and disconcerting, immensely demanding.'[83]

VENICE'S POWER was based from the beginning on its skill in building and sailing ships. For centuries the Arsenal was the foundation and backbone of the city's naval supremacy. Its beginnings were modest. The first shipyard was built around 1100 in the eastern area of the city called Castello – there was enough space there, next to monasteries and vegetable gardens, on difficult, that is, marshy ground. But the Arsenal grew rapidly. Venice's demand for ships was immense: the Republic needed merchant vessels, but more especially warships. The city was not exactly squeamish in her fight for control of the sea, hijacking the cargo ships of her competitors, or raiding their settlements on land. Time and again the Venetians launched campaigns of revenge and plunder. Even once she had become the strongest sea power in the entire Mediterranean, Venice still had continually to defend her position.

The Arsenal only really became a centre of the city's politics and economy in the fourteenth century, when the state took over its supervision. Henceforth, as the state shipyard for both military and merchant vessels, it was a government priority. *La Serenissima* invested her capital, her know-how and her energy into expanding and modernising it, thus creating the world's first ever integrated industrial complex. Everything was in one place: workshops, docks, warehouses, equipment suppliers. The city hired the best craftsmen, the most capable engineers and the most experienced seamen and put them to work together. The result was the first workplace in Europe with a developed division of labour. As in a modern factory, the *arsenalotti* (= everyone employed in the Arsenal) worked together in groups: carpenters, sawyers, caulkers (who sealed the hulls of ships with tar, one of the hardest jobs), apprentices and labourers were formed into appropriate teams guided by a chargehand and with a foreman in overall control. The Venetians built three large galleys every year, and prepared each completed ship for the sea on a kind of assembly line. As if on a conveyor belt, the ships were equipped with sails (stitched or repaired by women working in the Arsenal) and ropes (for which there was a huge fabrication building, the *tana*), as well as the essential and renowned Venetian ship's biscuit, from, needless to say, a bakery in the Arsenal. A galley could be sent on its way within a few hours. At its greatest extent, in the sixteenth century, the Arsenal employed up to 16,000 people and the site in its entirety covered one seventh of the surface area of the city.

The government accounts for 1423, under Doge Tommaso Mocenigo, show just how important ships were to the state. The city's budget was not measured in gold or land. The unit of currency

was the ship: 300 large trading ships with a load-bearing capac-
ity of up to 150 tonnes and 8,000 seamen, 3,000 small ships with
17,000 men and 45 galleys carrying 11,000 soldiers. The Venetians
were immensely proud of their Arsenal; they celebrated it as an
emblem of their prudence and skilful government. It made a strong
impression even on their competitors. Shipyards across Europe were
named Arsenal – originally an Arabic word, meaning 'the house of
craftsmanship' – after Venice's example.

When we read about Venice's eventful history as a sea power, we
are in fact reading alongside Rilke. The German literature archive in
Marbach holds a voluminous collection of the poet's notes, mostly
on Venice in the fourteenth century. Between 1910 and 1912, during
the change of direction that followed his completing *Malte*, Rilke
wanted to write a biography of Carlo Zeno, a fairly obscure admiral
who in 1380, in the so-called Battle of Chioggia, saved Venice from
its closest rival, Genoa.

Rilke began his studies in Venice in 1910. One Comandante
Malagora 'received [me] with perfect helpfulness and exactly in the
way required in order not to discourage a poor, ill-educated poet
who makes books because he does not know how to deal with those
that already exist. I am in excellent hands and am already about to
begin poking away in various libraries and, if my courage does not
fade, perhaps will stay here for three or four more days.'[84]

We do not know which libraries Rilke visited, though presum-
ably he went to the State Archive on Campo San Polo and to the
Biblioteca Marciana, Venice's chief library, and perhaps to the Biblioteca Querini-Stampalia, which we will come to on this walk. What
is certain is that, over the winter of 1911 to 1912, he read everything
he could find on the subject in the baronial library at Duino. He
had almost become a 'historian', he proudly reported in March
1912 to his friend Baroness Sidhonie Nádherni von Borutin: 'I am
reading in Italian, Muratori, for seven or eight hours every day, and

something to complement it in between, almost always on four-teenth-century Italian history, with particular reference to Venice. It is really so close, this unfathomable, and the library here teems with literature on the lagoons, the Adriatic, Istria and Friuli. [...] I want to get to the point where I really know something about this one state; it is the empire whose progress I believe I may fully see, the trajectory of its existence is purer than the meshed pathways of other polities, – a coherence which forms on earth what in heaven would be a constellation. How wondrously grandiose that it arises from the refuge offered by a couple of poor, marshy islands, and that *exactly that* which afflicted it has become its eternal glory. How could this not grip me over and over again?'[85]

Sometimes Rilke copied out quantities of facts and dates directly from Muratori (1672–1750), the standard work on Italian history, at other times he translated and summarised. He noted down battles, coups d'état, sieges, alliances, betrayal, murder and corruption, in chronological order, everything exhaustively considered, with comments and footnotes. He referenced numberless locations and names; he even drew out family trees. Only on Carlo Zeno is there nothing. Rilke did not write his biography. He was already in doubt about the project even while he was researching: 'This schoolwork is a kind of refuge for me from the vicissitudes of creative labour, which I don't feel I can truly cope with, as well as a discipline, which reins me in.'[86] From the great writing crisis that followed the com-pletion of *Malte*, even the sometime saviour of Venice could not save him.

The work of another great poet tells us about the Arsenal in the fourteenth century, the period, that is, which especially interested Rilke: Dante's *Divine Comedy*. You may read the Italian text on a tablet to the left of the Arsenal's imposing entrance gate. In English it runs:

In the vast and busy shipyard of the Venetians
there boils all winter long a tough, thick pitch
that is used to caulk the ribs of unsound ships.

Since winter will not let them sail, they toil:
some build new ships, others repair the old ones,
plugging the planks come loose from many sailings;

some hammer at the bow, some at the stern,
one carves the oars while others twine the ropes,
one mends the jib, one patches up the mainsail;

here, too, but heated by God's art, not fire,
a sticky tar was boiling in the ditch
that smeared the banks with viscous residue.[87]

An ugly place, Dante's Arsenal: it is in Hell and crooks and traitors
are stewing in the boiling sea of misfortune described here.

Today we can only discover how the Arsenal really looked from
plans, photos and pictures. Except for during the Biennale art exhibition, it is mostly closed. In Rilke's time, you could visit every day
except Sunday, from 9am until 3pm. It was even possible to inspect
the docks, with permission from the Admiralty.

We can nonetheless still gain an impression of the Arsenal's place
in the city's social structure. Castello is a workers' district of narrow
streets and small houses – and one of the earliest examples of social
housing. Here the city provided the *arsenalotti* with small dwell-
ings, in some cases for life. On the one hand, as we read in Dante,
the craftsmen of the Arsenal had very hard work to perform. On the
other, they were a kind of elite, an institution, their own stratum of
the city, with their own dialect and their own privileges, such as pen-
sions for life. The *arsenalotti* provided the police service in their own

district and guarded the Arsenal as well. That they formed the guard of honour for the Doge's Palace and on state occasions were allowed to steer the *Bucintero*, the Doge's huge ceremonial ship, added to their identification with the power of the state. You may inspect a model of that impressively decorated ship, along with 25,000 other exhibits on the history of seafaring and shipbuilding in Venice at the Museo Storico Navale, the museum of naval history, in the vicinity of the Arsenal.

The Scuola Dalmata di San Giorgio degli Schiavoni

The only tourist attraction in the area to the west of the Arsenal – the Scuola Dalmata di San Giorgio degli Schiavoni – is also of interest to Rilke enthusiasts. Here hangs the only cycle of pictures by Carpaccio to remain in its original location, a small chapel. On his first stay in Italy Rilke was planning a biography of this Venetian Renaissance artist, but he soon shelved the idea. He had Malte, the protagonist of his novel, write a book about him instead: 'I am twenty-eight, and have achieved next to nothing. Let us recap: I have written a study of Carpaccio, which is bad, a play, which is called *Marriage*, and which attempts, by suggestive means, to demonstrate something untrue, and verses.'[88]

Carpaccio is known as the great storyteller among painters. His subjects are religious or mythical, but in his saints' tales and legends (among them the stories of the Dalmatian saints George, Jerome and Triphon) he reproduced the world of his own time, down to the finest – often idealised – detail. His painting serves a single aim: to glorify his home city. The real protagonist of his art is always Venice. Carpaccio cast a glow over Venetian life in his paintings, above all through his subtle use of colour. In Rilke's words: 'The pictures of Carpaccio, if you have seen them, are as though painted on crimson velvet, something warm, one might almost say woody, breaks over everything, with listening shadows crowding around the subdued lights.'[89]

Labyrinths

It is easier to get lost in Venice than in almost any other city, on account of the dense, tangled web of *calli* (singular *calle*), as lanes and alleys in Venice are called, which often end in cul-de-sacs, or semi-private internal courtyards. Getting lost is part of the Venice experience. Even a native Venetian like the Princess von Thurn und Taxis did it sometimes, for example if she ventured into a working-class part of the city like Castello. She tells us about a 'strange experience' she had with Rilke on the way to Santa Maria Formosa, where our walk also ends: 'One fine morning we were going to the Stampalia gallery and Sta. Maria Formosa. I knew that Sta. Maria Formosa stands not far from S. Zaccaria, and must be very near to Riva dei Schiavoni. So, first by vaporetto (alas, the gondolas are becoming ever scarcer!) and then by foot. A small, obliging old man, who was roasting excellent chestnuts, showed us what direction to go in, "and then straight on!" Naturally, we should have gone in the opposite direction – and soon we were lost in a labyrinth of streets, alleys, bridges and sottoportici; a scandal for a Venetian like me! And then suddenly we found ourselves in such a strange and unfamiliar place ... A long street (not exactly what one calls in Venice a "calle") with a small fountain at each end and large, very tall buildings on both sides, – glum, plain houses without the grotesque ornamentation and open-work windows which one sees in the poorer areas of Venice, and a silence – a silence which seemed to have reached us from a vanished age [...]. The two of us stood there motionless and, with the same feeling of uncanny trepidation, looked at the broken pavement with grass (grass in Venice!) growing through the cracks, the closed, dumb, mournful houses, the barred windows, where no one showed themselves, the street empty of people. [...] We searched in vain for the name of the street, which is normally always written up, I believe we will never find that corner again [...]. We often discussed the episode. Rilke always insisted that in spite of all his searching he was never again able to find that weird street.'[90]

Pinacoteca Querini-Stampalia

The Pinacoteca Querini-Stampalia, which, in spite of everything, Rilke and the princess did in the end find, is among the less spectacular of the city's museums, but it is still worth seeing. Rilke also recommended it. This Renaissance palace houses more than four hundred paintings of the Venetian school. Though they may not belong to the first rank, they afford us nevertheless a good insight into everyday life in the city, particularly in the extensive collection of paintings by Gabriele Bella. The courtyard garden, laid out in 1963 by Carlo Scarpa, Venice's great museum architect, is also worth a look. It is an urban oasis of splashing water. For the diligent, the building holds a vast library with unorthodox opening hours. Rilke himself would have been able to work there until midnight. Count Giovanni Querini-Stampalia, its benefactor, gave his books to the city in 1868 on condition that the library would be open in the evenings. It remains so to this day: only on Sundays does it close early, at 7pm.

Santa Maria Formosa

Campo Santa Maria Formosa is connected to the Palazzo Querini-Stampalia by a small flight of stairs, also designed by Carlo Scarpa. Today the Campo is no longer a lonely square but reassuringly busy, and not just with tourists. Here we find the church of the same name, which Rilke immortalised in the first Duino Elegy:

But hark to the suspiration,
the uninterrupted news that grows out of silence.
Rustling towards you now from those youthfully-dead.
Whenever you entered a church in Rome or in Naples
were you not always being quietly addressed by their fate?
Or else an inscription sublimely imposed itself on you,
as, lately, the tablet in Santa Maria Formosa. [91]

'Lately' was, as already mentioned, 3 April 1911 – the day when Rilke and the princess still found the church after their 'strange experience'. The inscription, which 'imposed itself' on him, is located on the tomb of Gulielmus and Antonius Hellemans, two businessmen from Antwerp, who died prematurely ('immatura morte') in Venice at the end of the sixteenth century. If one believes the Rilke expert Jacob Steiner, the inscription adds 'nothing specific to the sense of the First Elegy'.[92] Should you want to read it anyway, you will find it in the right-hand transept of the church. The tablet hangs above the south door, beneath the sarcophagus.

The Ghetto

'EVERYTHING ONE CAN say about Venice has been said and printed,'[93] complained Goethe in 1786. But the master was wrong. One hundred years later, a young poet discovered a place that writers had ignored, travellers had avoided and the Venetians themselves had forgotten for centuries: the Ghetto. In 1900 Rilke became the first person to make it into a setting for literature, in one of his *Stories of a loving God*. 'A Scene from the Ghetto in Venice' tells of the love between the Venetian aristocrat Marcantonio and the beautiful Jewish woman Esther, who lives in the Ghetto with her grandfather Melchisedech. Rilke narrates in the style of a fairytale, and, at the end, a religious parable. At first the Ghetto functions merely as a backdrop for the allegory. But this appearance is deceptive. Rilke's little story will still serve on the streets of the city today to take you on a journey of discovery. His narrative turns out to be a useful travel guide into the most obscure corners of Venice's history.

There are two possible routes. For the first, follow Rilke's own directions in the story: 'If one travels under the Ponte di Rialto, on past the Fondaco de' Turchi and the fish market and then says to the gondolier, "Right!", he will look rather astonished, and ask sharply: "Dové?" Insist however on going right, disembark on the narrow, dirty canals, bargain with him, curse him and then walk through the

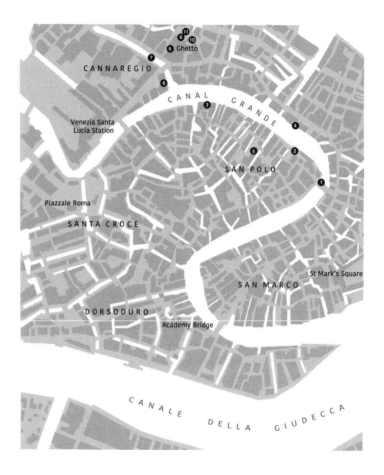

[1] **Ponte di Rialto** [2] **Pescheria** [3] **Fondaco Tei Turchi** [4] **Ca' d'Oro** (Gall'eria Franchetti) [5] **Palazzo Mocenigo** (Centro Studi di Storia del Tessuro) [6] **Palazzo Labia** [7] **Canale di Cannaregio** [8] **Ghetto Nuovo** [9] **Ghetto Vecchio** [10] **Ghetto Nuovissimo** [11] **Campo di Ghetto Nuovo**

cramped alleys and black, smoke-filled gateways out onto an empty, spacious square.'[94] Apart from the order (from the Rialto Bridge one comes first to the Pescheria, then the Fondaco dei Turchi) this still works. Nowadays you would probably take the vaporetto (route 1 to San Marcuola or route 52 to Guglie) to gain direct access to the Ghetto.

I propose, however, that we take a detour, as the story itself does. Rilke does not plunge straightaway in medias res. His story begins with a framing device, because he does not see the Ghetto as an isolated part of Venice, but rather situates it concretely in its surroundings, bringing together the various aspects of the city: contemporary reality, the historical and the artistic. These he confronts with the dark, other, forgotten side of the city, the Ghetto. On the one hand are well-known sights, resonant aristocratic names, glittering history and wealthy palaces; on the other, the Ghetto, right next door. By tracing out the two sides of the story and the city in one walk, we can appreciate how close they are.

The three palaces described below lie on our route into the Ghetto. They each repay a visit, and anyway belong to any programme of seeing Rilke's Venice.

Ca' d'Oro

My walk, like Rilke's story, sets off from one of the most prominent tourist emblems of the city, the Ca' d'Oro. The story begins with a conversation between the arrogant first-person narrator, in whom one may easily recognise the young poet, and Herr Baum, a typical tourist, the kind we all want not to be. They fire phrases at each other like ping pong balls. '"The Ca' d'Oro", – I gave back, "The fish market –" "Palazzo Vendramin –" "Where Richard Wagner" – he added quickly, being a cultured German. I nodded: "Do you know the Ponte?" He smiled, well oriented: "Of course, and the Museum, not to forget the Accademia, where a Titian ...'"[95] It is by now clear, if it wasn't before, that Herr Baum has understood nothing of the real Venice, into which the storyteller will soon lead him for the first time.

Most tourists only know the beautiful gothic façade of the Ca' d'Oro (built 1421 to 1434), which used to be covered with gold leaf, hence the name (*oro* = gold). That it has been possible, since 1900, to view the façade and the palace in something like their original condition, the city owes to a Jew, Baron Giorgio Franchetti. He bought the building in 1894, after it had become entirely run down and been mutilated by misguided restorers. The previous owner, a Russian prince, had demolished its famous staircase and had had all the marble decoration removed from the façade and floors. Franchetti restored everything to its original state, going so far as to use the old building techniques, so that the mosaics were, as formerly, cut by hand rather than by machine. Rilke met Baron Franchetti in 1911. Franchetti was friendly with the Princess von Thurn und Taxis and often visited her at Duino Castle. The poet found him a strange figure: 'In Venice, at the end of November, I saw Franchetti and listened to him play on an old harpsichord; he is a peculiar personality, half temperamental, half virtuoso and perhaps abused by both, a kind of brilliance.'[96]

Rilke did however have absolute respect for the Baron's commitment to the Ca' d'Oro. 'One may even walk into the Ca' d'Oro, which Baron Franchetti has had very judiciously restored: the little courtyard, the wondrous Byzantine stone fountain, the staircase and the view from the window like looking through luxurious lace, make a visit worthwhile.'[97] Still true today. You may also see Franchetti's private art collection – which was at the beginning of the twentieth century one of the most important of its day – and is still in the same state as when Rilke saw it and admired it. It contains a great deal of Christian religious art, such as a very beautiful 'Saint Sebastian' by Mantegna.

Palazzo Mocenigo

Rilke's story is set in the past, 'perhaps under the Doge Alvise Mocenigo IV'.[98] Does anyone know where he lived? We can find out. His portrait hangs in the Palazzo Mocenigo, today open to the public as a museum of textiles and costume. In the *portego*, the imposing entrance hall with its gallery of ancestral portraits, that patrician family shows what it had and what it was: a dynasty of rulers, which on its own supplied seven Doges. Each one of them is dressed in gold and crimson, proud and severe. Alvise IV (the one with the ermine) hangs to the right of the entrance, on the opposite wall. He was Venice's last Doge but one and ruled from 1763 to 1778, just before the end of the Venetian Republic.

It is worth taking a walk through the museum, though it is all rather dusty and old-fashioned. In fact, this is very much to its advantage, because everything originates from the eighteenth century, so it enables us to see how a family of grand Venetian aristocrats lived, from their salons to their boudoirs, during the time of Rilke's story. The exhibits are charming too, though not exactly laid out according to the latest ideas in museum design: the finest Venetian lace, filigree fans, expensively embroidered fabrics – Rilke would undoubtedly have loved these displays. Indeed, he himself assembled similar showcases at Duino Castle of 'tous les petits objets de la femme', seeking out the exhibits – fans, make-up pots, perfume bottles and small porcelain figures – from all over the house, rummaging in old cases and fetching things from the basement. 'Rilke was very proud of his work.'[99]

Palazzo Labia

Rilke would not be Rilke if in a text about Venice he did not write about art. So too in 'A Scene from the Ghetto': 'in the period I am talking about, people loved light paintings, on a ground of white silk, and the name that people bandied around, which beautiful lips threw up to the sun and charming ears caught when it fell quivering back down, that name is Gianbattista Tiepolo.'[100]

Tiepolo (1696–1770) was the last great Venetian painter. The most beautiful of his frescoes are to be seen in the Palazzo Labia, a pretentious baroque palace from the eighteenth century. The Labias were not an old-established family, but they were extremely rich. For the decoration of their first-floor ballroom, they hired Tiepolo, Venice's star painter, to paint something historical. And he did so – he painted the story of Antony and Cleopatra – but how! He combined a unique homage to his wealthy clients with mythological figures, trompe l'oeil architectural features and splendidly coloured allegories. The overall effect is sensuous, blithe, effortless. It is one of the most beautiful examples of how Venice's painters continued to paint the city with such charm, even at the very moment of its decline. Today the palace belongs to RAI, the Italian state TV broadcaster, and may be viewed only by appointment.

The Ghetto

Head out from Palazzo Labia, over a narrow bridge, take a few steps along Canale di Cannaregio and straightaway you are standing in another world. Through 'cramped alleys and black, smoke-filled gateways' – Rilke's description holds good today – you have arrived at the world's oldest Ghetto.

Throughout Christian Europe people had been trying to isolate the Jews since the twelfth century. But Venice was the first city that from the beginning of the sixteenth century forced its Jews to live in an entirely separate and strictly guarded zone. The chosen area was the remotest and dirtiest part of the city: the so-called Ghetto Nuovo, an area of disused cannonball foundries. This is probably the origin of the word 'Ghetto': in Venetian dialect, foundries are called *gèto*, factories where metal is cast, from *gettar* = cast.[101]

It was an ideal place to corral people, as a glance at a map of the city shows. This 'island' was surrounded on all sides by canals and, with only two bridges leading onto it, was very simple to guard. The gates on the two bridges were shut each night and guards patrolled around on boats (which the Jews themselves had to pay for).

In 1516, 700 families were forcibly relocated to the Ghetto Nuovo. In spite of the 'Nuovo' in the name, this was the original Ghetto. In 1541, when the previously untouchable rich Jews had to move into the Ghetto, the Ghetto Nuovo was enlarged to include an older foundry area, the Ghetto Vecchio. The Ghetto expanded for the third and final time in 1633 – adding the Ghetto Nuovissimo.

In spite of these enlargements, there was from the beginning very little space. The population density was three times as high as in comparable Christian districts. The result was an architectural peculiarity that you may also read about in Rilke's story: 'the Venetians [...] repeatedly reduced the area of the Ghetto, so that the families, who multiplied fruitfully in the midst of all their afflictions, were compelled to build their houses upwards, one on the roof of another. And their city, which did not lie on the sea, overflowed slowly into the sky, as if into another sea, and around the square with the fountain the precipitous buildings soared upwards on all sides, like the walls of some giant tower.'[102] The 'square with the fountain' is the Campo di Ghetto Nuovo – a good place to read Rilke's story. Here, and in the surrounding streets, one may still see the buildings with their very un-Venetian six or seven storeys.

In those days the Jews were not allowed to buy the houses in the Ghetto, which the Christian landlords shamelessly exploited and demanded rack rents for. But the Jews did have a kind of long lease and were allowed to build extensions. The only way to go was up. In Rilke's story this peculiarity of Ghetto architecture is more than mere local colour: it forms part of the unusual storyline. 'Wealthy Melchisedech, with the whimsicality of a very old man, made a disconcerting proposal to his fellow citizens, children and grand-children. He wanted always to live in whichever was at any particu-lar moment the highest of those narrow buildings, which hauled themselves up over each other in numberless storeys. People were happy to comply with this curious wish, because they had already lost faith in the load-bearing abilities of the lower walls and built the higher storeys of such flimsy stone that the wind seemed not to notice the walls at all. So the old man moved house two or three times a year and Esther, who did not want to leave him, always went too.'[103] Melchisedech is the grandfather of the beautiful Esther and the real protagonist of the story. He never sets foot outside the Ghetto, 'even though, as a goldsmith and someone who enjoys uni-versal respect, he could risk doing so.'[104] He has organised his whole life within the Ghetto and his faith.

This is historically realistic. Within the Ghetto walls, the Jews could arrange their own lives. A kind of mini-Republic. For example, the city allowed them to set up synagogues, whereas previously Jews could only meet in private houses. Life in Venice's Ghetto must have been intensely religious, as there were five synagogues for the various denominations within a very small area. Clearly the place the Jews had originally occupied for negative reasons had come to mean something different to them, as the American sociologist Richard Sennett explains: 'The formation of the Jewish Ghetto tells the story of a people who were segregated but who then made new forms of community life out of their very segregation'.[105] A two-sided process: over the course of time, the Jews were ever more harshly bullied out of Venetian life, while they, of necessity, turned ever more inwards. Rilke describes this too. When her noble lover tells the beautiful Esther about his everyday life, it sounds to his listeners like a travelogue from distant and exotic lands: 'Here Marcantonio sits at the feet of the aged Jew on a cushion embroidered with silver and tells stories about Venice, as if they were fairy tales which never happened exactly like that anywhere. He tells of plays, of the battles of the Venetian army, of foreign guests, of pictures and ornamented columns, of the "Sensa" on Ascension Day, of Carnival and of the beauty of his mother Catherina Minelli. [...] To his two listeners, everything is foreign; because the Jews are strictly excluded from all contact [...].'[106]

Why did a city like Venice, where foreigners had lived and conducted business for so long, become the first in the world to set up a Ghetto? This is Rilke's answer: 'Whenever a calamity befell the city, the people took it out on the Jews; the Venetians were much too similar in spirit to need the Jews for doing business, as other peoples did. They plagued them with taxes, robbed them of their merchandise, and repeatedly reduced the area of the Ghetto [...].'[107] According to Sennett, the founding of the Ghetto was indeed linked to a particular 'calamity', namely Venice's great crisis of political confidence at the beginning of the modern period. In the early years of the sixteenth century, Venice lost its monopoly over European trade. The Portuguese had discovered a secure sea route to India; the Turks had taken Constantinople in 1453 and threatened *La Serenissima*'s pre-eminence in the Mediterranean; and in 1509 Venice's attempt to establish itself on the mainland had collapsed miserably in an annihilating military defeat.

Such events within the space of a few decades shook the city's self-confidence. People sought for reasons, and found them in the city's debased and lax morality. Syphilis, which had been spreading rapidly across Italy and Venice in particular since 1494, served as a sign of this degradation. Syphilis, economic decline and political defeats: a scapegoat was required, and thus found, in a minority of whom Christians had long been suspicious – the Jews. On account of their religious practices (which no one really understood) the Jews were counted as unclean and this 'uncleanness' was considered to be contagious. However, the Jews were an important element in the urban economy. As the best bankers and moneylenders and as weavers, tailors and goldsmiths, they were vital for a city so concerned with pageantry and appearances. The Venetians neither wanted nor were able to expel the Jews. They cared too much about business. Ghettoisation seemed a prudent way forward. Having isolated the supposed source of contagion, the Venetians had symbolically restored the 'cleanness' of their city. At the same time they continued to profit from the Jews, as well as extorting ever-higher taxes and compulsory levies from them.

There was a great fear of physical contact with Jews in the city of globalised trade. It reveals itself in a characteristic detail: while the Christians sealed a deal with a kiss or a handshake, a contract with a Jew was concluded with a bow, at a proper distance. In Shakespeare's *The Merchant of Venice* (1596/97) this fear of contact plays a central role: the Jew Shylock agrees a curious contract with the merchant Antonio. If Antonio does not pay back the gold he has been lent, he will supply Shylock with 'an equal pound' of his flesh.[108] At first sight, the Christian Antonio appears to be an honourable man, because he gets into debt for a friend, while Shylock seems inhuman. At a superficial level, Shylock is exploiting his position to revenge himself on the arrogant Antonio, who has always despised him as a Jew. But hidden within this revenge is another wish, as Shylock reveals in the play's most famous speech: 'Hath not a Jew eyes? Hath not a Jew hands, organs, dimensions, senses, affections, passions?'[109] Shylock wants to be recognised – not just as party to a contract, but as a whole man, who can also be touched.

The fear of contact with the Jews showed itself in another way. The Jews were allowed to leave the Ghetto during the day, but so that people could recognise them and avoid contact with them, they had to wear a sign. It was in yellow, a low-status colour, which the prostitutes had also had to wear at times. Male Jews received a yellow badge – an early forerunner of the Nazi's yellow Star of

David. Still harsher strictures were placed on Jewish women, who could wear neither jewellery nor expensive clothing, only – like the prostitutes – a yellow scarf. As a result, Jewish women never felt safe on their own and seldom emerged from the Ghetto, even when accompanied. They rapidly almost completely disappeared from the Venetian street scene. Jewish women became a great enigma to Christians – and an ideal screen on which to project all manner of desires. Around 1600 an English traveller managed to observe the women in a synagogue in the Ghetto: 'I saw many Jewish women, whereof some were as beautiful as ever I saw, and so gorgeous in their apparel, chaines of gold, and rings adorned with precious stones, that some of our English Countesses do scarce exceed them'.[110] Jewish women awoke great lusts, but Christians were forbidden to have contact with them and love relationships could be severely punished. That in Rilke's story the nobleman Marcantonio is risking his life to visit the beautiful Esther in the Ghetto at night is entirely faithful to history.

Rilke's story is in any case not a story of carnal seduction, neither in one direction (sensual Jewess seduces Christian) nor in the other (debauched aristocrat seduces innocent Jewish girl). It is true that Esther has a child by Marcantonio, but it is rather a kind of immaculate conception: 'She had looked at him so strongly and for so long in the hours she had been alone with him, that it seemed to her as if he had already fallen deep into her dark eyes and died, and was now beginning, actually within her, that new eternal life in which he as a Christian believed. With this new feeling in her young body, she stood for days on the roof and sought out the sea.'[111] So the focus is precisely not on sensuality (which Jews were credited with), but on the spirit, which here the Jews incarnate. Rilke's story transcends the divisions between religions. For Esther, for her blonde, delicate child and for the old man Melchisedech, the Ghetto opens itself up to heaven.

In reality Napoleon's troops opened the gates of the Ghetto in May 1797, ten to twenty years after the time when the story is set.

By Rilke's lifetime, most of the affluent Jews had moved out of the Ghetto. Many Jews had seized upon Italian reunification in 1871 as a chance to break out of their isolation. They considered themselves to be Italian citizens and belonged to the new cultural elite, which pushed energetically for progress and modernisation. Giorgio Franchetti, for example, had not simply inherited his money from his mother (she was a Rothschild by birth), but had successfully invested in the expansion of the rail network and new productive cropping systems in agriculture. Even in Venice Jews had a decisive role in these changes – in the expansion of local transport and the building of luxury hotels on the Lido for example. Jews also now bought famous but often dilapidated palaces, which they previously would not have been allowed to enter.

Some, like Signor Grossini, father of Margherita Sarfatti, Mussolini's Jewish mistress, had an unsentimental attitude. Grossini was the first person to install a private lift into a historic palace, the Palazzo Bembo. Baron Franchetti by contrast gave the Ca' d'Oro to the city of Venice in 1927, along with all its furniture and his art collection – after he had paid for the expensive restoration work. As it happens, the Baron himself never wanted to live in the Ca' d'Oro. 'It was too good for him, Franchetti the Jew,' Rudolf Kassner wrote; 'it was meant for Doges and the like.'[112]

By the beginning of the twentieth century, only the poorest lived in the Ghetto. It was still overcrowded and was home to many small shops and businesses. Whoever was looking for second-hand goods or furniture and did not have much money, shopped there – as Rilke did, when he was setting himself up in the princess's *mezzanino*. But the Ghetto still did not belong to the city. Even for long-established Venetians it was terra incognita. In June 1912 when Rilke organised an expedition into the Ghetto 'with Countess Wallis, her cousin the

Countess Amélie Lippe and the little, inwardly seething Comtesse', he wrote to Marie von Thurn und Taxis: 'The face of the little one is so splendidly arranged for driving away smells, you may well imagine how much opportunity to deploy it she had in that milieu.'[113] Clearly it was the first time these aristocratic women had come into contact with that 'milieu'. Countess Wallis was, by the way, a Mocenigo by birth, descendant of the Doge during whose time in office Rilke's Ghetto story is set. Now here is the story:

A Scene from the Ghetto in Venice

Herr Baum, homeowner, chairman of the borough council, honorary chief of the volunteer fire brigade, and various other things – or, to be brief, Herr Baum – must have overheard one of my conversations with Ewald. Which is no great miracle; he owns the house where my friend lives on the ground floor. Herr Baum and I have known each other by sight for quite a time. But recently the chairman of the borough council has taken to pausing and raising his hat a fraction, as if to allow a small bird to fly out, should one happen to have been imprisoned therein. He smiles politely and initiates our acquaintance: 'Do you travel much?' 'Oh yes –' I responded, somewhat abstractedly, 'I would think so.' He continued in a confidential tone: 'I believe that we are the only two here who have been to Italy.' 'Well then –' I was struggling to be a little more attentive, 'then we really absolutely must have a talk.'

Herr Baum laughed. 'Yes, Italy – she really is something. I am always telling my children about her –. Take Venice for instance!' I stopped: 'You remember Venice?' 'Oh please!' he groaned, being too fat to express his outrage without some effort, 'how could I not? Whoever has once seen her – The Piazzetta – Isn't that right?' 'Quite so,' I replied 'I have especially fond memories of travelling along the Canal, gliding quietly, noiselessly along the border with the past.'

'Palazzo Franchetti,' he threw in. 'The Ca' d'Oro,' – I gave back, 'The fish market –' 'Palazzo Vendramin –' 'Where Richard Wagner' – he added quickly, being a cultured German. I nodded: 'Do you know the Ponte?' He smiled, well oriented: 'Of course, and the Museum, not to forget the Accademia, where a Titian ...'

Thus had Herr Baum undergone a kind of examination, a pretty rigorous one. I was determined to repay him with a story. I began without further ado:

'If one travels under the Ponte di Rialto, on past the Fondaco de' Turchi and the fish market and then says to the gondolier: "Right!", he will look rather astonished, and ask sharply: "Dové?" Insist however on going right, disembark on one of the narrow, dirty canals, bargain with him, curse him, and then walk through the cramped alleys and black, smoke-filled gateways out onto an empty, spacious square. All of this for the simple reason that it is there that my story takes place.'

Herr Baum touched me gently on the arm: 'Excuse me, what is this story?' His little eyes flicked anxiously back and forth.

'My dear sir,' I soothed him, 'it is just a story. Nothing important. I can't even tell you when it takes place. Perhaps during the reign of the Doge Alvise Mocenigo IV, though it could have been somewhat earlier or later. The pictures of Carpaccio, if you have seen them, are as though painted on crimson velvet, something warm, one might almost say woody, breaks over everything, with listening shadows crowding around the subdued lights. Giorgione painted on dull, ageing gold and Titian on black satin, but in the period I am talking about, people loved light paintings, on a ground of white silk, and the name that people bandied around, which beautiful lips threw up to the sun and charming ears caught when it fell quivering back down, that name is Gianbattista Tiepolo.

'All of which has nothing to do with my story. My story concerns the real Venice of palaces and adventures, of masks and pale nights on the lagoon, nights like no others anywhere, nights humming with secret romance. – In the part of Venice where my story is set there are only meagre everyday noises, the days follow one another monotonously, as if there were only one, and the songs one hears are laments that grow without ever soaring, settling over the streets like billowing smoke. At the first signs of dusk, timid, ragtag hordes wander the streets, numberless children make their homes on the squares and in the cold, narrow doorways, and play with the very same shards and offcuts of coloured glass flux from which master craftsmen pieced together the severe mosaics of San Marco. Few nobles ever enter the Ghetto. At most, when the Jewish girls gather around the water fountain, one may sometimes notice a black figure in a coat and mask. There are those who know from experience that this figure carries a dagger hidden in the folds of his clothing. Someone claims to have seen the face of this young man by moonlight, and has ever since insisted that this slim, black visitor is Marcantonio Priuli, son of the Proveditore Nicolò Priuli and the beautiful Catharina Minelli. He has been seen to wait under the gateway to Isaac Rosso's house, until he is alone, whereupon he crosses over the square and enters the house of old Melchisedech, the wealthy goldsmith, who has many sons and seven daughters, and many grandchildren from them. His youngest granddaughter, Esther, is waiting for Marcantonio, clinging to her aged grandfather, in a dark, low room full of glinting and shining things, where silk and velvet hang delicately over the vessels, as if to subdue their vigorous golden fire. Here Marcantonio sits at the feet of the aged Jew on a cushion embroidered with silver and tells stories about Venice, as if they were fairy tales which never happened exactly like that anywhere. He tells of plays, the battles of the Venetian army, foreign guests, pictures and ornamented columns, the "Sensa" on Ascension Day, Carnival and the beauty of his mother Catherina Minelli. For him, all these things have a similar meaning, varying expressions of power and love and life. To his two listeners, everything is foreign, because the Jews are strictly excluded from all contact and even wealthy Melchisedech never enters the realms of the Grand Council, even though, as a goldsmith and someone who enjoys universal respect, he could risk doing so. Over his long life the old man has secured many concessions from the Council for his fellow believers, who think of him as a father, but he has also experienced the backlash, over and over again. Whenever a calamity befell the city, the people took it out on the Jews; the Venetians were much too similar in spirit to need the Jews for doing business, as other peoples did. They plagued them with taxes, robbed them of their merchandise, and repeatedly reduced the area of the Ghetto, so that the families, who multiplied fruitfully in the midst of all their afflictions, were compelled to build their houses upwards, one on the roof of another. And their city, which did not lie on the sea, overflowed slowly into the sky, as if into another sea, and around the square with the fountain the precipitous buildings soared upwards on all sides, like the walls of some giant tower.

'Wealthy Melchisedech, with the whimsicality of a very old man, made a disconcerting proposal to his fellow citizens, children and grandchildren. He wanted always to live in whichever was at any particular moment the highest of those narrow buildings, which hauled themselves up over each other in numberless storeys. People were happy to comply with this curious wish, because they had already lost faith in the load-bearing abilities of the lower walls and built the higher storeys of such flimsy stone that the wind seemed not to notice the walls at all. So the old man moved house two or three times a year and Esther, who did not want to leave him, always went too. In the end they were so high up that when they stepped out from the corner of their dwelling onto the flat roof another country began at the level of their brows, and the old man would describe that country's customs in dark words, almost as if singing a psalm. It was now a long upward journey to reach them; the way led through the lives of many strangers, over steep slippery steps, past the scolding of wives and the ambushes of ravening children. Its many inconveniences limited their contact with the world. Even Marcantonio stopped visiting, and Esther hardly missed him. She had looked at him so strongly and for so long in the hours she had been alone with him, that it seemed to her as if he had already fallen deep into her dark eyes and died, and was now beginning, actually within her, that new eternal life in which he as a Christian believed. With this new feeling in her young body, she stood for days on the roof and sought out the sea. But, high though their dwelling was, she could make out only the gables of Palazzo Foscari, some tower or other, the cupola of a church, another cupola in the distance, as if freezing in the light, and then a lattice of masts, balconies, poles at the edge of the moist, trembling heavens.

'Towards the end of that summer, though the climb was very onerous for him, the old man ignored all protests and moved house again; someone had built a hut, higher than all others. As he was again walking over the square, after such a long time, with Esther supporting him, the people pressed around him, bowing over his fumbling hands and begging for his advice on many matters; because he was to them like a dead man who has risen from the grave, because a time has been fulfilled. And he looked like it too. The men told him that there was an uprising in Venice, the nobles were under threat and soon the boundaries of the Ghetto would fall and all would enjoy the same freedoms. The old man said nothing in reply, only nodded, as if he had known of these things and a great deal else besides for a long time. He entered Isaac Rosso's house, at the summit of which stood his new apartment, and climbed for half a day. Up there Esther bore a blond, delicate child. Once she had recovered, she carried it in her arms out onto the roof and for the first time let the whole golden sky fall on its eyes. It was an autumn morning of indescribable clarity. Objects grew darker, almost without glinting, except for lone flying lights that settled on things as if on huge flowers, rested a while, and then floated away over the gilt-edged contours into the sky. And there where they disappeared one could see from this highest of places what no one in the Ghetto had ever seen before, – a silent, silvery light: the sea. And only now, once Esther's eyes had become accustomed to this glory, did she see Melchisedech, standing on the very edge of the roof. He raised himself up with outstretched arms and forced his dull eyes to gaze at the day as it slowly evolved. He kept his arms up high and his brow was aglow with thought; it was as if he were making a sacrifice. Over and over he let himself fall forward and pressed his old head onto the roughly hewn stones. The people gathered together on the square below and looked upwards. Isolated gestures and words rose up out of the crowd, but none reached as far as the lone praying old man. To the people the very old man and his youngest looked as if they were in the clouds. For a long time the old man continued, raising himself up proudly and then in humility collapsing to the ground. And the crowd below grew and did not stop looking at him: Has he seen the sea, or God, the Everlasting, in his glory?'

Herr Baum struggled to say something quickly. He didn't immediately succeed. At last he said dryly: 'The sea, obviously – it is very impressive, after all' – thus proving himself to be a peculiarly enlightened and knowledgeable man.

I hastily said my farewells, but I could not resist calling back to him: 'Don't forget to tell your children about this incident.' 'My children?' he began. 'Don't you realise that this young nobleman, this Antonio, or whatever he's called, is not a nice character at all and besides: the child, this child! That really won't – for children –' 'My dear sir,' I reassured him, 'you have forgotten that children come from God! How could the children doubt that Esther received one because she lived so close to heaven?'

The children have heard *this* story as well and if you ask them what *they* think the old Jew Melchisedech was seeing in his rapture, they will reply without thinking about it: 'Oh, the sea too.'

A Tintoretto in the Madonna dell'Orto
Church and a poem by Rilke

THE MADONNA DELL'ORTO Church lies far out in the northeast of the city, but it is a must for Rilke fans. Here hangs a painting by Tintoretto that inspired one of Rilke's poems. Both poem and painting are called 'The Presentation of Mary in the Temple' (Presentazione di Maria al Tempio). Comparing the two is doubly enlightening: Rilke's poem helps you to understand one of Tintoretto's most beautiful pictures, revealing the particularities of his painting style, use of colour and composition. (With this in your armoury, you may also more easily appreciate Tintoretto's famous cycle of pictures in the Scuola Grande di San Rocco and his ceiling paintings in the Doge's Palace.) You could also hardly have a better insight into Rilke's working methods, learning how Rilke 'built' his poems and what role images play in them.

My suggestion: read the poem first; then look at Tintoretto's painting in the church, while keeping in mind Titian's painting on the same theme, which we already saw in the Accademia.

The Presentation of Mary in the Temple
To grasp how she was then, try if you can
to place yourself where pillars mount to ceilings

[1] Church Madonna dell'Orto [2] Casa Tintoretto [3] Campo Santa Maria
Formosa [4] SS. Giovanni e Paolo [5] mooring Madonna dell'Orto

which are in you; where you can share the feelings
of steps; where arches take great risks to span
the gulf of inward space you could not part with,
since it was made of such huge blocks to start with,
heaving it from you would have meant the fall
of your whole being: if you'd had the strength.
When you are stone-filled, when you've reached the length
of being just vault, vista, entrance, wall –
seize the great curtain hung before your face,
hiding the gleam of objects so exalted
breathing is checked by them, blind groping halted:
try, with both hands, to pull it back, a trace.
High, low, near, far, palaces fill the place;
banisters stream, as stair from stair emerges,
broaden, then balance on such dizzy verges
you're seized with vertigo. Near things efface
their outlines in the cloud of smoke that surges
from burning censers; but each levelled ray
from those far off makes for you, straight and lancing, –
and if clear light from fire-bowls should be dancing
on robes that very slowly come your way:
could it be borne?
She came though, and she raised
her eyes, and stood there taking it all in.
(A child, a little girl between grown women.)
And went up to the pampered splendour then,
(it swayed a little) calmly, quite undazed:
so far was all that had been built by men
inferior to the voice that praised
within her heart. And the desire
to go by inner signs, by these alone.
Her parents thought they lifted her; the one,

so menacing, whose breast flashed jewels' fire,
seemed to receive her: but she went through all,
the child, out of their hands into her fate,
prepared already, higher than the hall,
pressing more hardly than the building's weight.[114]

Rilke's poem is part of his now less popular cycle 'The Life of Mary'. In thirteen poems he presents the stages in the life of the mother of God, from birth to death. The individual episodes derive from the *Legenda Aurea*, a thirteenth-century chapbook containing lives of the major saints. The primary purpose of the legend of Mary was to show that the future mother of Jesus was holy in her own right from birth. So it is in the episode represented here: because Anna and Joachim had been childless for a long time, they made a pledge at Mary's birth to devote their child's life to the service of God. When their daughter was three years old, they sent her to the temple. As the temple had been built on a small rise, little Mary had to contend with fifteen steep steps – so the *Legenda Aurea* precisely records it, at any rate. Quite exceptionally for a child of her age, Mary climbs the steps unaided, alone and full of confidence. Already, as a small child, she is a saint. The book is clearly Rilke's source for the legend. But the decisive stimuli for his arrangement of the material came from two Venetian paintings: 'Many of the details and the arrangement of this sequence of images are not my invention; in little Mary's climb up to the temple, you may without difficulty recognise echoes of Italian paintings (of the Titian in Venice's Accademia, for example, and especially of the thrilling Tintoretto in Santa Madonna dell'Orto.)'[115]

The most prominent echoes are in the architectural detail. The poem abounds with words to do with architecture and space, which Rilke has taken from the two paintings – the columns from Titian for example, the balustrades from Tintoretto. But the tone of the poem as a whole comes from Tintoretto. With the Titian the observer remains outside and distanced. Rilke draws the reader straight into the poem, addressing them as 'you' and making them a part of the story, inviting them to imagine 'where you can share the feelings / of steps; where arches take great risks to span / the gulf of inward space' – just as Tintoretto uses the perspective of the thrillingly foreshortened steps to draw the viewer right into the picture, so that they 'feel' how steep and vertiginously high the steps are. Tintoretto was a master of this kind of foreshortened perspective. Self-taught (Titian had thrown him out of his studio as soon as he recognised his apprentice's talent), he developed his own painting methods, making jointed mannequins out of wax, suspending them in mid-air and then studying them from different angles.

In one other vital way Rilke is nearer to Tintoretto than Titian: in his representation of Mary. In the Titian, Mary, the steps, the priests and the temple take up only half the picture. The real focus is on the gaudily dressed onlookers on the other side. Here Titian depicts numerous prominent and aristocratically dressed Venetians, including members of a wealthy fraternity, his clients. He had no choice. In the Tintoretto, the flight of steps takes up the bulk of the picture, which nevertheless stealthily focuses on Mary, small and far in the distance though she may be. A shaft of light leads our gaze up the steps to Mary's little figure. Completely bathed in bright light, she glows against the dark of the other figures. This too was a speciality of Tintoretto, who was famed for his chiaroscuro, the use of gleaming lighting effects to achieve dramatic emphasis.

Rilke masterfully translated Tintoretto's artistry into his poem – using unusual linguistic means. He puts Maria into a parenthesis: '(A child, a little girl between grown women.)' A parenthesis in a sentence normally contains an interesting but irrelevant addition. By using brackets in a poem and putting Mary between them, Rilke turns this role on its head: the parenthesis becomes a subtle exclamation mark, delicately emphasising the fact that Mary is really still a child as she walks fearlessly up to the priest, 'the one, / so menacing, whose breast flashed jewels' fire'. (This priest is also easy to spot in Tintoretto's painting.) The poem is more than a description of the picture. Rilke uses language to create his own architecture, his own space, in which the essence and drama of Tintoretto's picture are preserved.

THE QUESTION REMAINS, what in the figure of little Mary so interested Rilke? For Titian and Tintoretto, religious subjects were part of their daily bread. But Rilke was a modern poet. He rejected the Catholic Church all his life and Mary here is not another one of his unhappy female characters. On the contrary, she knows her purpose, her fate. She is small but strong and has 'the desire / to go by inner signs, by these alone.' The 'I' of the poem watches her security and pleasure almost enviously, as if he would take her place. This 'I' is not longing for religion, but for clear inner certainty of his own fate as an artist, of his task as a poet and his dedication to the pleasure of linguistic signs. Unlike Mary, the poet is not standing on high, in bright light, but – like us – watching from the bottom of the steep flight of steps. He stands alongside us in the here and now of life, facing the heights, whether of religion or art. As a modern poet, Rilke must cross that dizzying gulf in his writing, over and over again, without Mary's religious certainty.

THE OTHER PAINTINGS by Tintoretto in the Madonna dell'Orto Church are also worth seeing. He painted most of them for free for his parish church. Just nearby, at Fondamenta di Mori Nr 3399, is the house where he lived most of his life. Jacobo Robusti, son of a silk dyer – hence his nickname Tintoretto – was an outsider to the guild of artists, always controversial. El Greco, whom Rilke also valued highly, was one of the few painters to study with him. Tintoretto died in 1594. He lies buried with his family in Madonna dell'Orto.

YOU COULD VISIT the church and Tintoretto's house after the Ghetto walk. Or you could find them from Campo Santa Maria Formosa, as Rilke did: 'And this morning I was very proud to have made the journey: Sᵃ Maria Formosa, S.S. Giovanni e Paolo to Madonna dell'Orto without a single wrong step, led by my quiet instinct.'[116]

One option for the return journey would be the vaporetto from Fondamente Nuove to San Marco. The trip along the eastern edge of the city gives you an excellent sense of the extent of the Arsenal.

Behind the backdrop –
Palaces on the Grand Canal

O N HIS FIRST DAY in Venice, 28 March 1897, straight after
his arrival at around 6pm, Rilke embarked on a 'trip along
the Canal Grande past the famous Palazzi Vendramin and
Papadópoli'.[117] He wrote about it the same day: 'We travelled the
length of the Canal Grande in a gondola. – This portrait gallery in
stone made an overpowering impression on me. All the names of
proud families, which had resonated seductively in a boy's distant
dreams, Dándolo and Vendramin, Venier and Mocenigo, Loredan
and Contadini, Grimaldi and Falieri – all woke again to consciousness at the sight of the palaces, in whose silent rooms the fastness of
their power shimmered – it was a strange, deep joy, a serious pleasure, which I will not forget for a very long time.'[118]

A trip on the Grand Canal is one of the most beautiful ways
to experience Venice, no matter whether by gondola, the express
vaporetto route 82, which does not dock at every stop, or the slow
vaporetto route 1. It is lovely every time, day or night. The splendid palaces line themselves up, one after another, over four kilome-
tres. Here the richest and most powerful families in Venice built
their residences. It is a museum of Venetian architecture from every
period, and a beautiful backdrop. But what is played out behind the

[1] **Hotel d'Europe** (Ca' Giustinian) today it is the venue of the Biennale [2]
Grand-Hôtel Britannia (Palazzo Tiepolo-Zucchelli) today: Hotel Regina
e Europe [3] **Hotel Regina** (Rome e Suisse) today no longer a hotel [4]
Grand-Hôtel (Palazzo Ferri-Fini) today no longer a hotel [5] **Church Santa
Maria della Salute** [6] **Palazzo Barbaro-Wolkoff** [7] **Palazzo Dario** [8]
Casetta Rossa (Casina delle Rose) [9] **Ca' Mocenigo Vecchia** [10] **Palazzo
Mocenigo** [11] **Palazzo Barbarigo della Terazza** [12] **Palazzo Papadopoli** [13]
Palazzo Bembo [14] **Palazzo Vendramin** [15] **Hotel Luna** [16] **Hotel Bauer**
(Grünwald) today: Hotel Bauer

scenes? How did people live in such palaces in Rilke's time? Which palaces did he know and where was he a guest?

Luxury hotels

The first palace on the Grand Canal that Rilke entered was his hotel: the Grand Hotel Britannia in Palazzo Tiepolo-Zucchelli, just in front of St Mark's Square and the Royal Garden (Giardinetto Reale) on the same side of the Canal. In those days the Britannia was one of the city's three top-of-the-range hotels, with a lift, central heating, a garden and 235 rooms. Fine writing paper, printed in England, was available gratis. The view was too: 'We sat, as yesterday, on our hotel balcony, which reaches right out over the Grand Canal. The starry night hung in gentle folds over Santa Maria della Salute, like a white, miraculous dream, and the broad black waterway melted away into infinity beyond the weary lights.'[119] Today the hotel is called Europa e Regina and still offers a superb view from its terrace restaurant directly on the water, looking out over the Salute Church (and Palazzo Cini, formerly Valmarana). It was already expensive in Rilke's time, but the poet had a wealthy sponsor. He was the guest of Nathan Sulzberger, a Jewish chemistry student from New York, whom he had met in Munich. On 2 April 1897 Rilke sent 'loyal words of joy and thanks from my whole heart for those precious days' to his 'young American friend', along with an edition of his book of lyrics *Dream-crowned* with a dedicatory poem. Then he broke off contact. Not until 1920 did he recall his friend: 'Venice wants to be "believed", when I first saw it, I happened to be the guest of an American!'[120]

After that, Rilke paid for his hotels in Venice himself. They all stood near the Britannia, on the same side of the Grand Canal, except for the Hotel Luna, where he spent a few days in 1911 – not far away, almost on St Mark's Square, and nothing awful, but a 'rather less exacting' establishment, eleventh in the Baedeker rankings. (Today it is a five-star hotel.) Right on the Grand Canal is Hotel Regina, where Rilke stayed (today no longer a hotel), and the Grand Hotel in Palazzo Ferri Fini, where Rilke came twice from Duino, at the end of November 1911 and in March 1912, and on one occasion with his great love 'Benvenuta', Magda Hattingberg, in May 1914. Rilke liked the Grand Hotel, and visited it often to eat, even when he was not staying there. At the Grand Hotel he even allowed himself to get carried away drinking wine: 'And do you know what took my fancy there – just today, all over again – jusqu'à la folie?: Your splendid Orvieto. We first tried it on the evening before the departure of Princess T. (...) but that was not the right location. At the Grand-Hôtel it is seduction itself ...'[121]

The best hotel that Rilke stayed in was the Hotel de l'Europe (ranked number two in Baedeker) in the Ca' Giustinian, today the offices of the Biennale. Franz Grillparzer, Verdi, Wagner and Théopile Gautier all stayed there. In June 1920 Rilke wrote: 'The Europe has nearly ruined me (even though I have never eaten there).'[122]

Palazzo Barbarigo della Terrazza

A little further along in the direction of the Rialto Bridge, on the opposite side of the canal, near the San Tomà landing stage and next to the mouth of the Rio San Polo, lies Palazzo Barbarigo della Terrazza (today a German study centre). Rilke visited it in November 1907: 'You should have seen the light of a Venetian afternoon on these Flemish tapestries in the endless mirrors, reflecting each other, and the ornate, wood-carved frames which have grown into them in their baroque opulence. And there are the long galleries with their tall portraits of purple cardinals, crimson procurators and rigid, iron generals, underneath whom a heavy white horse lifts up its hoof. And to step out from such a room onto the marble terrace – you may well imagine how much it means to me.'[123]

Rilke may perhaps have been thinking here of his novel *The Note-books of Malte Laurids Brigge*. One scene in the book takes place in a Venetian salon, possibly inspired by the Palazzo Barbarigo. This quotation is well known, but generally only its second half, in which Rilke offers a poetic description of Venice. In the first half, however, the poet rails bitterly against Venice's tourists:

'That was in Venice, in the autumn, in one of those salons where foreigners temporarily gather together around the lady of the house, who is as much a foreigner as they are. These people stand around with their cups of tea and are in raptures whenever a knowledge-able neighbour quickly and discreetly points them towards the door in order to whisper them a Venetian-sounding name. They are pre-pared for the most outlandish names, nothing can surprise them; as they are so frugal with their experiences elsewhere, in this city they blithely abandon themselves to the most exorbitant possibilities. In their regular existence they consistently confuse the extraordi-nary with the forbidden, and, having allowed themselves to expect something miraculous, their expectation manifests itself as a gross, debauched expression on their faces. What they experience at home only for a moment at a concert, or when they are reading a novel alone, they display in these flattering surroundings as if it were a legitimate state for public view. Just as they allow themselves, quite unprepared and perceiving no danger, to be egged on by the music's almost fatal confessions, as if by carnal indiscretions, so they sur-render themselves, without mastering Venice's existence in the least respect, to the gondolas' rewarding swoon. The no longer newly-weds, who have exchanged only spiteful ripostes their whole journey, sink into taciturn tolerance; the man is overcome by the bland wea-riness of his ideals, while she feels young and nods encouragingly at the languid natives, smiling as if her teeth were made of sugar that is forever disintegrating. And then one hears, it turns out they are leaving tomorrow or the day after tomorrow, or the end of the week. [...] Before long, it will be cold. The supple, narcotic Venice of their preconceptions and demands disappears with the somnolent foreigners, and one morning the other city is there, real, awake, brittle to the point of shattering, absolutely not what was dreamed, willed in the middle of nothing on sunken forests, forced, and, at last, absolutely present – Venice. The hardened body, reduced to the bare minimum, through which the unsleeping Arsenal compels the blood of work, and the insistent, ever expanding spirit of this body, stronger than the scent of aromatic lands. The suggestive state, which exchanged the salt and glass of its poverty for the treasures of nations. The beautiful counterweight of the world, that, even in its decoration, is full of hidden energy, branching out ever more finely – : this is Venice.'[124]

Palazzi Mocenigo

When Rilke wrote this passage he was himself a stranger in Venice. Just a year later he belonged to Venetian 'society'. In her *Reminiscences* Marie von Thurn und Taxis writes: 'He felt contaminated by the Venetian languor and moaned a little about insurmountable joylessness and continual fatigue. So he lived from day to day, an existence as if "amongst reflected images", avoided foreigners, who bored him intensely, but happily from time to time saw the ladies of Venetian society in splendid old palaces, particularly in one, where Lord Byron had once stayed and where the amiable hostess charmed him with her beauty and courtliness.'[125] This lady was descended from a family whose resonant name had already made an impression on Rilke on his first gondola journey along the Grand Canal: she was one Countess Mocenigo.

As well as the Palace that is today the museum of costume, her family owned three richly decorated buildings on the Grand Canal, the Ca' Mocenigo Vecchio and the two Palazzi Mocenigo, diagonally opposite the Palazzo Barbarigo della Terrazza. Lord Byron lived in one of these palaces from 1818 to 1819 and the family had kept up the tradition of literary salons into Rilke's time: 'I saw him [the Russian painter Alexander Wolkoff-Mouromtzoff, also known as A N Roussoff] yesterday at Countess Mocenigo's. I pushed myself to approach him, at first it was very cosy, then there was suddenly such an abundance of people that he and I quietly made to go. In the beautiful dark front room Countess Valentine stopped me and resolutely brought me back again. She did so in her imperious and entirely genial way, she is taking me, it seems, under her wing, and wants to read my poems on the spot – but I am a little frightened by her as well. [...] The Countess Mocenigo both appeared and was so effortless that it is difficult to describe.'[126]

By 1920 Rilke's report of an evening at the salon sounds entirely different: 'You are not allowed to make contact, you enter, you walk around, you drink small garish drinks – it is fundamentally as boring as any place where society pretends to wallow in its own amusements, which are nothing but habits.'[127]

Palazzo Barbaro-Wolkoff

The Palazzo Barbaro-Wolkoff, a delicate red building from the Renaissance, stands on the same side as the Palazzo Barbarigo della Terrazza, in the direction of St Mark's and just before the Santa Maria della Salute Church. Rilke came here often as a guest in the early summer of 1912. The then owner, the Russian painter Alexander Wolkoff-Mouromtzoff, who had inherited the palace, belonged to that small number of men with whom Rilke had a close relationship. Rilke had met him in Duino and both were passionately interested in contemporary art. In May 1912, Rilke paid him an 'inaugural visit': 'I was at Wolkoff's for a lengthy evening, he spoke, wanted some kind of proof of my existence from me, I recited "The

Panther", very badly as it happens, with the feeling one has when one shows the doctor one's tongue.'[128]

They met each other regularly, at the Countess Mocenigo's salon as well, but it was not a simple relationship. 'There was a short brawl with Wolkoff yesterday about Cézanne,'[129] Rilke reported to the princess. This was unusual for the placid poet, who elsewhere – if one believes Rudolf Kassner – 'rarely had a discussion of any kind'.[130] The arguments didn't bother Wolkoff: he invited Rilke to live with him. 'The day before yesterday he had the idea to show me round his house, the beautiful room upstairs, and suddenly he was giving me ever more instructions, how best I could go about using it. Yesterday it became apparent that he was entirely serious, and would not take "No" for an answer, his last word was that he hoped I would come later if that suited me best –, and today he is leaving. Faced with this new temptation to vainglory, I take refuge with you [...].'[131] It was less vainglory than common pragmatism that deterred Rilke. He preferred to live with the princess than that difficult man, as she correctly saw: 'But when Wolkoff, being very insistent and brooking no refusal, invited him to move into his charming little palace on the Grand Canal, our poor friend became almost sick with fear and wrote to me immediately in order to know if he could take refuge in my apartment.'[132]

Eleonora Duse, the most famous actress of the time, did however live there, in exactly the beautiful room that Wolkoff showed to Rilke. She rented the apartment from 1894 to 1897, as even the Baedeker used to record. There is a portrait of her from that time, painted by Wolkoff, who was quite besotted with her. (His only good picture, the princess once sardonically remarked.)

Eleonora Duse was one of Rilke's great idols – until he met her in Venice in 1912. Their encounter was one of the great but exhausting experiences of that artistically meagre summer. The Italian writer Carlo Placci, another member of the princess's Duino circle, arranged for them to meet, on 1 July: 'I want quickly to tell you the most beautiful thing: Duse wanted to see me, I did nothing towards it, though meeting her has been one of my great wishes for ten years; now it has happened, without anyone thinking of it, by itself, like one of those things that follow the pace of the stars among us, almost without knowing us. And she lives a few steps from my house, we see each other a great deal, and when at peace, she is indescribably patient of humanity, which allows these hours to be exactly that which they always could have been.'[133]

Rilke had been daydreaming about the actress for a decade. As a young man he had even dedicated a play to her, *The White Princess*. It was never performed. Indeed, Rilke's theatrical career was brief and only modestly successful. His love of theatre and his admiration for Duse remained, however. For him the actress was the epitome of the tragic, not only for her unique skill as an actress, but also because of her love affair with Gabriele d'Annunzio, in which all of Europe shared. It was a Venetian love story, which began in May 1894 in the luxury Danieli Hotel (where d'Annunzio was staying) and ended in 1900 with a literary scandal. They were a contrasting couple: the younger, highly ambitious poet, until then rather better known for his numerous amours, and the sober, world-famous actress. It was a great passion and a fruitful artistic collaboration – mostly for him. He wrote plays especially for her; she financed the lavish productions. She lost her entire fortune in the process, because his dramas did not really work on stage and were only made bearable by her formidable skill as a performer. When d'Annunzio abandoned her for a young Roman aristocrat, Duse first learnt about it from a newspaper. And worse was to come: the writer snubbed her publicly, painting a crude portrait of her as an ageing diva in his erotic novel *The Fire* (1900). 'He has paraded me like an animal at market,' Duse wrote to a friend.[134]

A woman who is both a victim and a remarkable artist – that had to appeal to Rilke. In 1905, while he was Rodin's secretary, he had written her a letter, which the diva had not answered. In 1906 Rilke diffidently asked Karl von der Heydt to arrange for him to meet her. Duse was staying in Berlin to give a guest performance and was the celebrated star of the time. But von der Heydt did not plead for his friend and, besides, Rilke had toothache and couldn't go out, so again the meeting did not happen. After so many attempts, it's understandable that the poet should have reacted so enthusiastically: 'We were like two bowls and formed a fountain on top of each other and showed one another only how much perpetually escapes us. And yet it was inevitable that we should somehow communicate to each other the glory of being so full and perhaps we even thought in the same moment of the vertical living stream, which rose above us and (always, over and over) fell and filled us so completely –.'[135] The princess's reaction to Rilke's letter was restrained: 'I am very pleased that you have met Duse – I can imagine you so well – completely entranced of course – that woman was created to bewitch a poet.'[136] Privately she thought otherwise: 'I was calm, when suddenly an unexpected catastrophe hit – in the form of Eleonora Duse! Now poor Serafico would have no more peace; he was straightaway drawn into her magic circle. [...] I knew Duse well. I had seen her in moments when she had poured out her whole heart to me. A wondrous, formidable being but – a hopeless one. A sick, ageing, deeply unhappy woman.'[137] Nevertheless, the princess was naturally curious and so asked Rilke: 'Be nice Dottor Serafico and write to me often about her. Kassner would also have loved to meet Eleonora dalle belle mani [...].'[138]

Rilke and Duse met daily during July: 'Duse came to me often then – she lived very nearby, I could spot her from my writing desk as soon as her gondola turned from the lagoon into my canal.'[139] The actress was living not in the Palazzo Barbaro-Wolkoff but somewhere on the Zattere near the mezzanine. She often invited the poet over for supper; they chattered; went on outings; toured around in a gondola. Always present was Lina Poletti, a young feminist writer and Duse's lover (in her letters, the princess contemptuously refers to her as 'Mrs P'), who had been writing a play for Duse for years. Alexander Moissi, the star actor of Berlin's Deutsches Theater and famed for his Hamlet, sometimes shoved his way in. He was supposed to be recruiting Duse for Max Reinhardt's theatre. A vivacious, loud man, he was too loud for Rilke: 'Moissi ... rushes in, penetrates, overwhelms.'[140]

But it wasn't only her entourage that disturbed Rilke. Duse herself did. Being 54 years old, she did not, upon closer inspection, fit his ideal: 'Cowardly as I now am, I scarcely dare to look at her; it gives me a kind of pain to find her so broad and robust, this reinforced body, like a setting from which the stone has already fallen. I am so afraid of seeing her disfigurement, or simply something which is no longer there, that I can remember almost nothing except her mouth [...]. And the smile of course, surely one of the most famous which has ever been smiled [...].'[141] Besides, Duse was a true diva: she bitched and put on airs; she aborted their outings without warning because a peacock had frightened her; and one night she simply vanished. 'Rilke was sick with anxiety. Next morning Duse had returned.'[142] Rilke was touchingly concerned for her (he could be that too!), going so far as to help her find somewhere to live. But wherever they were, Duse griped: 'She is wearing herself out, letting her own body fall into disrepair [...]. We have not found the house she imagined, and it only takes half an hour for her to wear out an apartment, even the ceiling is no longer acceptable. At certain moments there flows from her an unwillingness to exist so piercing that it is as if everything around her has had its teeth fall out –'[143]

As an artist, Rilke admired her attitude of disappointed love. Day to day, however, it was hard to bear. She was constantly arguing vociferously with her young lover because Poletti was making no progress on the script. Rilke stood between them, spoke with one and then the other, achieving nothing: 'Between the two there is always reproach and bitterness, melancholy and powerlessness, paralysing them both.'[144]

On 1 August 1912 the two women separated and went away. Rilke, completely exhausted, remained behind: 'Since the days of Duse, those exceptionally strange days, I have been pretty depressed,' he wrote to the princess. Her dry commentary: 'You should know, Dottor Serafico, that I am glad that both Duse and Poletti have pushed off – you would otherwise have been eaten as if by ants.'[145]

Later Rilke would on several occasions lobby on the actress's behalf, even trying to find sponsors for her – but he preferred to keep her at a distance. When Duse wanted to perform his 'Life of Mary' in a nun's habit, he refused in horror: 'Straightaway this idea really does not appeal to me.'[146] He never wanted to meet her again. In 1920 he wrote to Lou Andreas-Salomé: 'When, on top of everything, I learnt that Duse was coming to Venice, ill, in order to find somewhere to live, I was so terrified that this was now repeating itself as well, that I left within twenty-four hours and returned to Switzerland!'[147]

Casetta Rossa

Casetta Rossa lies almost opposite Palazzo Barbaro-Wolkoff, on the other side of the Grand Canal. The 'little red house', so called because of its façade in Pompeian red, belonged to the Prince von Hohenlohe, brother of the Princess von Thurn und Taxis. 'Rilke had made friends with my brother, who lived in a charming little house on the Grand Canal. We were his guests almost daily, in his pretty little dining room, decorated with old mirrors, which reflected his expensive porcelain with views of the Brenta villas and his old silver. Rilke was as excited by this as by my mezzanine on the other side of the canal [...].'[148] The Prince von Hohenlohe was expelled from Venice during the First World War as an Austrian and enemy alien and had to leave his beloved house. From 1915, he rented it out to an old friend, the poet d'Annunzio, who made it the private headquarters for his spectacular wartime exploits.

The 'Garden of Eden' on La Giudecca

O NE OF RILKE's favourite places in Venice was the 'Garden of Eden' on La Giudecca, which was in those days an insider's tip, unlisted in any Baedeker: 'Suddenly you come upon them, these gardens brimming over their ancient walls, which a poet (Henri de Régnier) rediscovered only a few years ago, after they had long been as good as lost. They have an indescribable secretiveness, and one imagines that the silence that pervades them must become stupe-fying; they are not large, and have no view, unless they lie on the lagoon, like the beautiful garden of that old Englishman (Mr Eden). You should try to land there en route to one of the islands (Giardino Eden, Giudecca; ask for permission at the gardener's shed).' [149]

A GARDEN IN VENICE? In the city of water, of marble, of stone upon stone? Whoever thinks Venice is not a green city has made a mistake: it's only that the gardens lie hidden behind high walls. Venice has a rich botanical tradition. In the sixteenth century it was the centre of horticultural research in Europe. Nowhere else were there so many of the then fashionable botanical gardens, experimental gardens planted with food crops and medicinal plants from the Orient, exotic fruit trees, herbs and vegetables. All the important Arab and

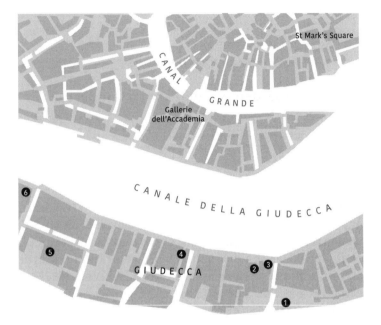

[1] **Giardino Eden** [2] **Church Il Redentore** [3] **Calle dei Frati** (the Calle dei Frati leads to the garden of the monastery) [4] **Trattoria Altanella** [5] **Convento delle Convertite** [6] **former Mulino Stucky**

Indian treatises on gardening were first translated in Venice. In the eighteenth century the owners replaced most of the fruit and vegetable gardens behind their palace walls with ornamental gardens in the baroque or rococo style, with their geometrically trimmed hedges, statues and fountains. In the nineteenth century everything was designed to be 'natural', in the style of the English garden.

Giudecca island – in reality eight small islands joined together by bridges – was already an important area for gardens in the sixteenth century, on account of its situation, far enough away from the bustling centre, but close enough for rapid access. The aristocracy built their summer residences here, with large parks and gardens for *la villeggiatura*, the holiday season. They accommodated their important guests here, and held noisy garden parties. Then, in the middle of the nineteenth century, the aristocrats retreated, abandoned their summerhouses and villas and allowed most of their gardens to fall into neglect. It was foreigners who revived interest in horticulture, foreigners like the Englishman Frederic Eden, who in 1884 purchased more than a thousand square metres on the Giudecca, where once there had been a fabulous park but were now only ruins, broken statues and grounds overrun with weeds. In a short time Eden succeeded in putting the garden back in order. By the turn of the century the Giardino Eden, as it was called in honour of its new owner, was again famous. Be they aristocrat, intellectual or artist, anyone who wanted to relax and who knew about gardens came. Rilke visited the garden whenever he spent time in Venice with the Valmarana ladies, the princess or Eleonora Duse, who particularly loved it.

However, the garden was already under threat again in Rilke's lifetime. As he wrote in 1920 to Nanny Wunderly: 'There is the garden that you should save, – because when its widowed proprietress dies, it is intended that factories be erected in its grounds (there have already been negotiations about it). The Giudecca, once

Venice's garden quarter, is already heavily industrialised [...].' [150]
This industrialisation was the reason why so many of the summer
residences had been abandoned. During the nineteenth century this
place of peaceful recuperation had become one of Venice's few areas
of modern industry. Breweries and liqueur factories grew up here
and industrial buildings increasingly reshaped the character of the
island. The most imposing example, and a source of great contro-
versy when it was built in 1895, is Molino Stucky, which was until
1955 Italy's largest flour mill and pasta factory. This huge building
lies across the water from the Zattere, roughly opposite the Pension
Romanelli. In 1907, Rilke would have had a very good view of the
hulking brick building. (Following years of neglect, it has now been
restored and reopened in 2007 as a Hilton hotel.)

The Giardino Eden was not in the end industrialised, but sur-
vived for decades as one of the great wonders of the modern gardener's art, until a storm surge of 1966 severely damaged it. Today it
is the largest private garden in the city and belongs to the Hundert-
wasser Foundation. The park again looks as it did in Eden's time – at
least what you can see of it. For you cannot go inside: you may no
longer enquire from the gardener, and the gate is firmly shut. It is
bordered on one side by walls and the canal, on the other by a prison
fence with a watchtower. (Another peculiarity of the Giudecca – in
the mid-nineteenth century several former monasteries there were
converted into remedial schools and prisons. What was once the
cloister of the Convertite on Rio delle Convertite, for example, is
today a women's prison.) To the rear of the Garden lies a grassed-
over square, and some dismal social housing.

So is it worth the journey? With Rilke in your bag, yes: 'Imagine
a flat garden (one travels to its gate along a silent, remote canal), with
arrangements and clusters of trees only at its edges, to the right and
left; save for two inconspicuous gardeners' sheds, there is neither
house nor pavilion within it, but stone figures are dotted around,

rhythmically spaced; they stand as if in a series of bosky intérieurs, obscured by the shifting shadows cast over them by the delicate June vine leaves in their genial arcades. In the innermost part of the garden, like a carpet, is a pool of verdant, cloudy water, framed in marble; bright flecks of matthiola, the stems of hollyhocks, roses, and the burning, blooming pomegranate bushes against the breezy, Tiepoloesque sky. In front of these green spaces, however, separated by old walls and sculpted hedges, a serious wide strip of lawn, alone, along the waters of the lagoon, a garden, strange, floating, a garden of sad freedom, if you will, a garden that remains empty, if one does not fill it with inner images and with longing. *You* would, Nike. And though it's not like an alleyway, if I were walking there noiselessly next to you, I would gently lay my arm on yours.'[151]

Little survives of the Giudecca's gardening history, but it is still possible to view the monastic garden next to the Il Redentore Church (which is busy in its own right, on account of Palladio). Here the Capuchin monks plant artichokes, cauliflowers and herbs, and grow vines, peaches and apples – just as they would have done in a medieval kitchen garden.

L'Altanella restaurant

Also on the Giudecca is the restaurant L'Altanella, already a good place to eat back in Rilke's day. D'Annunzio raved about the 'Sarde in Saor', sardines marinated according to a Venetian recipe, which taste particularly good here. Today the restaurant still serves classic Venetian food on a beautiful terrace by a quiet canal. It is worth a visit. A particularly good dessert is 'Uvetta alla Grappa', a small glass of raisins soaked in grappa.

The Lido

WHEN RILKE was having yet another writing crisis, or he was under stress, or the Scirocco was oppressing him, there was for him only one solution – board the steamboat and go to the Lido. 'I am not going to any churches or galleries, I am spending my entire afternoons outside along the Lido; at its furthest extent, by the San Niccolo Fort, a stone causeway reaches out for three-quarters of an hour's walk into the sea; you cannot always go on it, sometimes a guard prevents you, but whenever I can, I walk right up to its deep blue, spacious end, completely alone in a circle of glistening open-ness. It is a true victory.' [152]

Up until the mid-nineteenth century the Lido was scarcely more than an extended sandbank across the entrance of the Venetian lagoon. Many travellers to Italy from the North saw the sea here for the first time in their lives – as Goethe did, for example, in October 1786, and went quite into raptures over it: 'I set out early this morning with my guardian angel to the Lido, that tongue of earth that closes off the lagoon and separates it from the sea. [...] I heard a loud noise, it was the sea, and soon I saw it, the high waves were breaking on the shore as it withdrew, it was around midday, the time of the ebb tide. So I have seen the sea as well with my own eyes, and pursued it onto the beautiful threshing-floor that it leaves

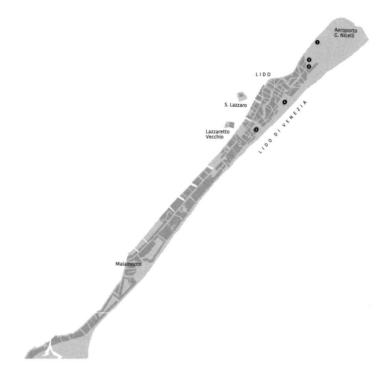

[1] Church San Nicolò [2] Cimitero Ebraico [3] Cimitero Cattolico [4] Hotel Des Bains [5] Hotel Excelsior

behind it as it yields. I wished the children were there, on account of the shells; I was like a child myself and picked up a quantity [...].'[153]

When Rilke described the Lido, 130 years later, the talk was no longer of an island in such a paradisiacal state of nature: 'Its views of course, and its natural situation, the Lido will never lose, but if you ask me how I find the island itself, as a place, my God, I wish I had known it fifty or sixty years ago, when it was still an area of open vineyards and fields, when the "countryside" of Venice really stretched for several miles from Malamocco to the point of San Niccoletto, whose brick façade is positioned to face directly west, in the evening it pushes outwards into the surrounding radiance and the gentle, slow reflection of space and object. Perhaps the square in front of the church retains something of what it once was, the little meadow next to it, where the gayest of public festivals have been celebrated for centuries, enveloped me recently in an unspoilt rural world and over it, golden, as if embroidered onto the sky, stands the as yet empty *albero degli amanti*, an immense plane tree, the likes of which for full-grown beauty I have only seen in the southern-most parts of France. If you go to S. Niccoletto and hunt for flowers in the grass, it could very well be times past, when it came as an enthralling surprise to penetrate into a copse along a thin footpath and to discover in the darkness, jumbled up amongst the brambles, old Jewish gravestones – which have now been put into banal, soul-less order, the Hebrew cemetery fenced in with a high unspeaking wall, all around is tidied up, empty, already on the way to becoming a building site. In fact, an appalling patch of villas has already sprung up not far away, on the city side of the Lido, right up to the beach, where large, monstrous, exorbitant hotels steal the air in a single swoop, stupid buildings, which look as if they have wolfed down thirty houses and become fat on them, each window fit to accommodate a single man, reproduced badly five hundred times. And in between are the banally planned modern military buildings,

dull, full of redundancy: enough, enough ... there remains, naturally, a good deal of splendid beach and even still some gardens, and
you may ride along the sea's edge, endlessly. (And the light, and the
gleam in the air!)'[154]

Rilke's assessment holds true in its essentials today: there is a large,
cordoned-off military compound around San Nicolò, and though
the Jewish graveyard has not become a building site it remains
fenced in, and there are many tarmac roads. Even the square in front
of the church is asphalted, empty and boring.

And the Lido's famous sandy beach?

Rilke loved the beach. Indeed, he rented a *capanna*, a typically
Venetian swimming hut: 'My life is turning out to be unbeliev-
ably provisional, – except that I have today taken possession of my
capanna on the Lido, so perhaps my life will become a smidgen more
definite.'[155] Rilke's *capanna* was obviously not just of existential significance: he used it for swimming as well. Rilke in a swimming
costume? Absolutely – ever since his summer in Wolfratshausen in
1897 he had taken care not only to eat a vegetarian diet but to do
ever more exercise as part of a healthy lifestyle, wherever he was. In
Berlin-Schmargendorf, where he lived in 1899, he happily chopped
wood and loved taking long walks, barefoot, through woods and
meadows. At Duino Castle he toughened himself up in winter with
a 'centaur's cure': air baths, which 'do you good from the body deep
into the soul'.[156] When in 1920 Venice's vaporetti stopped work the
poet complained bitterly: 'No news here, except that the vaporetti
have kept up their strike for a week, which is irritating inasmuch as
it would be very agreeable in this oppressive heat to be able to flee
to the Lido for a swim.'[157]

The fashionable beach life that had been typical of the Lido from
the mid-nineteenth century was never to Rilke's taste. He preferred
solitude. His *capanna* lay at the furthest end of the beach, away from
the to-and-fro of well-heeled tourists in the large luxury hotels. If

you want to know more about them, you had best read Thomas Mann, as Rilke did, obtaining a copy of *Death in Venice* as soon as it appeared in 1912. Within it, Thomas Mann turns his experiences on a swimming holiday at the Hotel des Bains in 1911, amongst other things, into literature: 'He [Gustav von Aschenbach, the protagonist of the story] had himself allotted to a rented beach hut, had a table and armchair set up out on the sandy wooden platform and made himself comfortable in the deckchair, which he had pulled towards the sea, onto the wax-yellow sand. [...] The grey, shallow sea was already alive with wading children, swimmers, colourful forms lying on the sandbanks with their arms folded under their heads. Others were rowing small keelless boats painted in red and blue and laughing as they capsized. In front of the extended line of capanne, on whose platforms one sat as if on a little verandah, there was energetic play and lethargic, stretched-out calm, visits and chit-chat, punctilious morning elegance alongside brash nakedness, comfortably enjoying the freedoms of the place.'[158]

Rilke, thrilled by these descriptions, praised the first part of the novel in the highest terms: 'Thomas Mann's Venetian novella, of which I as yet [...] only know the first part, has touched me wonderfully: the German is masterfully direct and for me, who have virtually become a Venetian, it has a special resonance.'[159] When he came to read the second part, however, his criticism was startlingly sharp: 'By way of contrast, consider this (do you think it is because of the moment when I got myself tangled up in it?), the second part of "Death in Venice" was to me simply embarrassing, I have not yet even had the courage to take it up again. Granted that this is how it had to progress, even in its calamitous unravelling and disintegration, whose phosphorescence is almost like a lone source of light in which what is playing itself out becomes visible – and that there were really no more details to be given, just fumes and smells and clouds, rubbing up against each other, I grasp all that, absolutely, and yet, I don't know, it is as if the reader had not been assigned anywhere to stand, somewhere from which he might be able to let himself like it all, the art of storytelling was so advanced in the first part that nothing more is told in the second, it flows and soaks everything and one watches as it spreads like spilt ink.' [160]

IT IS NOT SO EASY, one might add, for a tourist to hire a *capanna* today. Most of these little bathing huts have been firmly in the hands of Venetian ladies for generations. It's a real shame, because it would be a way to meet the old nobility, like the Contessa Valmarana, who hired a *capanna* in the most exclusive area, next to the Hotel Excelsior. For two months' use of a little wooden hut in the front row there one pays 7,000 Euros; at the Hotel Des Bains it costs 5,000; and even at the dowdier end of the beach, where there are no more hotels, you will still be paying 2,700 for a front-row *capanna*.

For those who want to enjoy something of the life of seaside luxury, I recommend hiring a deckchair and a sunshade from the Hotel des Bains. It's still expensive, but you can rent by the day, and then read your Rilke there – as Marlene Dietrich once did.

In 1937 Dietrich, no longer wishing to return to Germany from Hollywood on account of the Nazis, spent her holiday at the Hotel des Bains on the Lido. Her daughter Ruth Maria, her ex-husband Rudi Sieber and her ex-lover Josef von Sternberg were with her. One morning on the hotel's stretch of beach she met Erich Maria Remarque, who had achieved worldwide fame for his novel *All Quiet on the Western Front*. The Nazis had burnt his book in 1933, and though a Berliner by birth, he had, like Dietrich, lived in the USA ever since. Dietrich liked intellectual men, but Remarque had until now ignored the Hollywood star in his hotel. Dietrich: 'I had a book by Rainer Maria Rilke under my arm and was looking for a place in the sun where I could sit down and read. Remarque came up to me. He saw the title of the book and said in a rather sarcastic voice: "I see you read good authors." I responded with equal irony: "Should I recite a couple of poems for you?" He turned his perpetually sceptical eyes upon me. He didn't believe me. A film actress who reads? He was stunned when I then recited to him my favourite poems: "The Panther", "Leda", "Autumn Day", "Solemn Hour" and "Childhood". "Let's go somewhere else to talk," he said. I followed him. I followed him all the way to Paris [...].'[161]

Rilke was more to Dietrich than a means to her amorous ends. Like many of her generation she had idolised him since she was a young girl. It was in order to recite his verses that she actually first became an actress (or so she claimed, at any rate). Certainly there were nineteen volumes of Rilke's work in her extensive library. She read Rilke right up to the end of her life, buying a final book of his poetry in 1987. When she was in her eighties she proposed two recordings to a German radio broadcaster: 'Marlene Dietrich reads Jewish humour' and 'Marlene Dietrich recites from her favourite German authors, Goethe and Rilke'. The broadcaster, Freies Berlin, just wanted the Rilke, for $10,000. Whether that was too little money or the diva would only do the two projects together, Dietrich in the end never recorded a disc of Rilke's poetry.

Sestiere San Polo, the Frari Church and Ca' Rezzonico

RILKE WAS NEVER INTERESTED in the day-to-day life of the ordinary people of Venice: he was too concerned with the artistic character of the city. He didn't write a great deal about the more banal side of his own life either. Only with his last visit to the city, in the summer of 1920, did he describe a few small experiences: aimless walks, wandering around looking in shop windows, playing the lottery and shopping. Naturally even these notes are highly stylised. The poet never described something 'just as it was'. Rilke's sketches of Venetian daily life are usually virtuoso compositions, with the effect of painted vignettes: 'I "have seen", as people put it, almost nothing [...]. Now I can find no peace in my hotel room, I am driven through the narrow calli, over and under the stepped bridges, on which short, crook-backed Venetian women approach you in their black scarves, at first only half visible, like portraits on a base of translucent air, which deepens itself like the inside of a mirror in front of the wondrous red or black-and-white crumbling palaces, an unheard-of transparency, a scarcely more spacious dimension.'[162] Rilke almost never names particular places; you could not 'tick off' his mood pictures on an organised tour. Hence my suggestion: like Rilke, wander around an area aimlessly, perhaps San Polo, the smallest of Venice's districts (called *sestieri*).

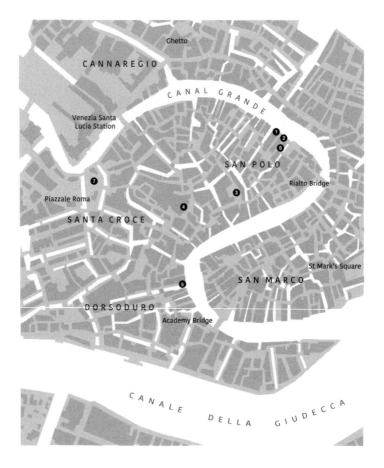

[1]Pescheria [2] Erberia [3] Campo San Polo [4] Church Santa Maria
Gloriosa dei Frari (I Frari) [5] Ca' Rezzonico [6] Bàcaro Do Mori [7]
Giardini Papadopoli

San Polo (which includes the Rialto Bridge) was formerly the centre of Venice's trade in high-value goods from the East: jewels, spices and silk. In the twentieth century many of these businesses were replaced by fruit and vegetable stores and souvenir stands. The fish market (Pescheria) and the vegetable market (Erberia) still remain, and make a good starting-point for a morning walk inspired by Rilke. After crossing Campo San Polo we will come to the Santa Maria Gloriosa dei Frari Church, which contains a famous Titian (with Rilke there is always art). Our walk ends in Venice's most beautiful museum, Ca' Rezzonico.

Erberia and Pescheria

One of Rilke's most beautiful texts from his last stay in Venice concerns the Italian art of decoratively arranging fruit. You may still admire this art today in Venetian markets like the Erberia and Pescheria: 'It's amazing that the fates who watch over us did not change me at that moment into a Venetian fruitseller, my love, *that* would be a job for me, watching over all these peaches and apricots, making sure they stay fresh until midday, and the swollen figs, which are already exhausted when they arrive: what a responsibility. What does one do to maintain an illusion of coolness in the minds of these decrepit fruit? Read them fairytales from Lapland? The Italians, who love every kind of "contrivance", set their fans whirring, like orators on a street corner, in some of the shops they fasten strips of paper to the demonically spinning wheels, so that they flutter horizontally out over the fruit, banishing the flies, – and in the back of this black, gloom-ridden boutique a whole system of air exchangers and movers appears to be in operation: real wind rushes out from where it has been lying hidden in ambush, the green leaves under their burden of fruit fold over and the shopgirl's hair, as on one of Goya's witches, is blasted about in front of her and almost out of the shop altogether. Really, though, the cool, transparent blackness in the depths of these humble shops is a wonderful thing, even a shop in the shadiest narrow calle manages to create within it another degree of murk, so that the fruits, as in an old Dutch painting, are not just colourful but seem actually to be glowing, as if they are really that room's stars and moon and quarters of the moon, releasing all the sunlight they have gathered in a single, intense burst. I have seen small, slender little carrots, marvelling at the cold, take on in this environment a pink of Manet-like delicacy, this basket of pale little roots was like a masterpiece of French or Spanish painting, with a little touch of the Neapolitan. And now imagine the life of a cat in such a lucid blackness, or the sudden upward glance of a Venetian girl, a salesgirl working in the shop, a moon over those moons, the gleam of the chosen fruit reflected in the pallor of her face and the mirror of her eyes.'[163]

Campo San Polo

Onwards to Campo San Polo, Venice's second largest square, which is surprisingly contemplative and not a particular tourist destination. In 1912 the Campo sparked off in Rilke some highly existential thoughts: 'Certain squares, such as the one directly in front of S. Pietro, and the great Campo S. Polo, where people hang out their washing, have an effect on me, as if I am looking at them through the eyes of childhood, they are so large, so old-fashioned, that I become small as I look over them, and somehow expectant, naïve; I can't describe it. [...] I am certainly now far more bound to it than I was –, and yet, when I consider living there, if I really think about it as somewhere to live, it melts away ... It is always still as if there were no more room for me, always the future is running away from me, like existence running away from the frog in the air pump.'[164]

Santa Maria Gloriosa dei Frari

Santa Maria Gloriosa dei Frari Church was one of the few tourist sights Rilke visited in 1920. Finally he was able to see one of his favourite paintings – Titian's 'The Assumption of the Virgin' – restored to its original surroundings, instead of in the Accademia. Another Madonna. In 1897 Rilke had praised it in the highest terms: 'The blessed one, on a wreath of clouds with cupids blossoming from its gentle waves, floats upwards into the vast spaces of everlasting radiance, where God-the-father awaits her purity in welcoming goodness. She rises easily, as if raised up by the flowing clouds into the sunny heights of her deserved transfiguration. In her upturned, wondering eyes, faith and thanks – and a certain curiosity about seeing the glory of heaven and of the creator who rains down blessings and her new home of eternal springtime. – Mary is not God's virgin, who at the dawning of some mystical longing seeks the Son on the right hand of the Father; she is the blessed woman who, from being in harmless error, returns to the naturally exalted state of noble womanhood; it is not the glow from yonder that makes the heaven of her eyes gleam and her lips smile; her own mercy, the sacrifices she has made with her own hands, have sanctified her. And so exactly those pictures which the church celebrates as the fruits of its deepest teachings are enemies of all Christian dogma and sun-filled witnesses to the eternal unrevealed religion of goodness and peace.'[165] Rilke's interpretation seems elaborate, but it becomes more plausible when one remembers what he is really talking about. The purpose of his first trip to Italy was his final initiation as a writer. He even named it 'his consecration as an accepted artist'. Although his text sounds quite religious, Rilke steals the religion from Titian's Madonna, he unchurches her, and in the same breath makes the woman he has profaned sacred as a mother. Titian's artistry gives the secularised Mary a new holiness. Not the church but the artwork reveals the 'eternal unrevealed religion of goodness'.

Almost a quarter of a century later, he sounds different, much more religious. But even now the religiosity is art's creation: 'In the Frari Church, next to the great "Madonna with the Pesaro family" [another painting by Titian] a slim aerial bomb has been hung up like a huge iron earring. It punched its way in nearby without doing any further damage. This church has received a new dimension, its height has become more rising, floating, heavenly, simply by virtue of the return of Titian's "Assunta" to the frame of the high altar. In the Accademia, where we knew it, this ascension of Mary had become an object of art historical erudition, it seemed one could see anything in it at all. Now, restored to the space for which it was first intended, it again unfolds the double miracle of Marian consummation and Titianic ecstasy, – the pure figure vaults away against the background of the choir, full of divine farewell, rises, surges, ascends and pulls the entire church upwards into the immeasurably opened blessedness of the ultimate heaven ...'[166]

Ca' Rezzonico

Our walk concludes at the Ca' Rezzonico, Venice's museum of the eighteenth century, most beautifully approached from the Grand Canal. Rilke spared no pains to get into what was then (in 1903) a privately owned palace. The English poet Robert Browning, husband of Elizabeth Barrett Browning, also a poet, had died there in 1889. Their love story was a dramatic one: in 1846 Elizabeth married her younger fellow writer in secret, because her father was against the match. Already sick, she eloped with Browning to Florence and died there in 1861, long before her husband. Such a woman's destiny naturally interested Rilke and he translated Elizabeth Barrett Browning's sonnets in 1908 – along with two Shakespeare sonnets, his only translations from English.

Rilke had encountered Elizabeth Barrett Browning in a book by the Swedish educationalist Ellen Key. He now asked if she might be able to help him: 'But today, very urgently, the question: is it possible to get into the Palazzo Rezzonico in Venice (we [Rilke and his wife Clara] will be spending two days there) and what must one do in order to gain such a privilege? [...] It would be a real joy to me, I am ready to see the portraits and possessions of the Brownings, on which your beautiful Life dwelled for a while.'[167] Ellen Key replied: 'You may try by asking with the porter at Rezzonico; you could say to him that you are a devotee of Browning – I believe that will work, with a Lira for drinking money! I can in future obtain permission through the Brownings, but there isn't time for that now.' [168] The Rilkes got in nevertheless: 'We were allowed into the Palazzo Rezzonico without further ado and wandered around full of justified gratitude. Filled as we were with the image of the poet couple (as your dear book has given it to us) we did not find the palace empty and the life that had quivered through it has scarcely yet died away. It was our best day in Venice, when the gondola brought us to the steps of this rich palace. It stood there, serious and lofty, and the red azaleas, blossoming a thousand times, waved in front of its high windows and shone like youth and eternity over the marble parapets ...'[169]

Today the Ca' Rezzonico is the Museo del Settecento Veneziano, the Museum of Eighteenth-Century Venice. It is a wonderful location to imagine oneself back into the eighteenth century, which Rilke so loved in the city. As he put it: 'If to everything one considers to be Venice, one adds, like a small, tender thoughtfulness, like a fragrance which makes a large gift more intimate and alluring, that which lingers in the air as the city's last living gesture, the Venetian dix-huitième: with its dark Pietro Longhis, its radiant Guardis, its always rather cloudy mirrors and the gentlemen and ladies, who meet and part, anonymous as madrigals, hidden under their baute [the traditional Venetian costume of hooded cloak and face mask], noiselessly gliding away from each other on gondolas. From this, from this final, self-exhausting pantomime, one may understand for certain the miracle of Venice [...].' [170] That sounds as if it might have been written specifically for the museum, but Rilke never knew it, as it did not open until 1936.

Many paintings that Rilke saw in other locations hang here, displayed in the splendid ambience of the 1700s. Work on building the palace began in the seventeenth century, but the architect Baldassare Longhena died and the owners went bankrupt. In the mid-eighteenth century, they sold the completed ground floor to the Rezzonicos, a very rich family who originated from Genoa. They had only just bought their way into the Venetian aristocracy for 100,000 ducats (at least two per cent of the state's entire income for that year) plus another 60,000 ducats of donations to good causes. They stopped at nothing in their work on the palace and hired only the best architects and interior designers. By 1756 it was completed. Just in time, for in 1758 Carlo Rezzonico was elected Pope. Under the aegis of Pope Clement XIII, as he named himself, the Palazzo became the centre of the city's culture, though not for any spiritual activities. The noisiest parties, the most colourful carnival fancy dress balls, concerts and theatre performances were held here. One can still catch a hint of this atmosphere today. In the great hall on the ground floor stands an exquisitely constructed gondola, such as every noble family would have once owned. Up the huge stone staircase one comes to the *piano nobile*, with its vast ballroom, decked out with swanky armchairs, vase stands and other spectacular furniture. In this ambience, the eighteenth-century pictures come into their own: an entire room of paintings by Pietro Longhi (1702–1785) shows small genre scenes of the daily life of ordinary Venetians, with carnival masks, as well as curiosities like a rhinoceros. Francesco Guardi (1712–1793) painted scenes of the upper classes: noble young nuns behind a grille, receiving their relatives in the cloister, and luxuriously hooded maskers, celebrating carnival in the gorgeous Palazzo Moisè.

Even the Venetian painter Rosalba Carriera, for whose pastel portraits Rilke had a particular weakness, is represented. (There are many of her pictures in the Accademia as well.) More significant as paintings are the vast ceilings by Gianbattista Tiepolo in the reception rooms on the first floor: yet more allegorical figures (Fame, Wisdom, Power and Virtue) in sensuous poses and fine silk robes that reveal more of the body than they conceal. Above all else, Tiepolo celebrated festive Venice – and of course his wealthy patrons, the Rezzonicos.

The Museum contains a chiaroscuro counterpart to this frothy rococo world: a room of frescoes painted by Tiepolo's son, Giandomenico, for the family's private summer residence, the Villa Zianigo. Father and son, who often worked together, created for their aristocratic clients 'light paintings, on a ground of white silk', as Rilke put it in his 'Scene from the Ghetto in Venice'. But for his client's private house Giandomenico showed another side of their world. White is still the predominant colour, but in sickly shades. In front of this pale backdrop cavort the crudely deformed, grotesques, hunchbacks with obscenely long noses, the haggard. The focus of many of the images is Pulcinella, the Neapolitan lout, one of the nastiest of the Carnival masks. Giandomenico Tiepolo's cycle of frescoes is more than just a comic caricature of the public world. It is a private record of the decline of the Republic in the eighteenth century.

An ombra in Bàcaro Do Mori

Whoever likes their food and drink more Venetian than Rilke did, and does not react so sensitively to noise, crowds or strongly flavoured food, can drop in to a bar for an *ombra* – a glass of wine – in the sestiere of San Polo. In these so-called *bàcari*, small local wine bars with simple food, of which there are several in this area, you drink a glass of white wine or prosecco (usually standing up) and, as Venetians do from late morning on, eat *cicheti*, small appetisers which come in many varieties. The Do Mori belongs among the oldest of the city's *bàcari* and serves Venice's best and freshest prosecco.

Farewell: San Giorgio Maggiore

R ILKE GAVE GISELA VON DER HEYDT some special advice for the
last day of her trip to Venice: 'Towards evening you must visit
San Giorgio Maggiore, the always palely shining moon that stands
opposite the sun that is Venice. And if it is one of your last days in
Venice, or indeed the last, climb the tower: stepping outside among
the bells hanging above you, you will see clearly in every direction
the glory stretching further than your eyes can reach. Here and there
you will be able to make out a dome, a tower, the gleaming face of a
façade. And everything will have a certain implausible quality, something unattainable, as if it were an illusion [...].'[171]

The little island of San Giorgio Maggiore lies opposite the
Piazzetta and the Doge's Palace, two minutes away by vaporetto.
Most tourists visit only the famous church by Antonio Palladio,
with its stunning late works by Tintoretto ('The Last Supper' of
1594 amongst them). More stunning still however is the view over
Venice from the Campanile. In return for a small contribution to the
Benedictine monks who operate the lift in the tower, one receives a
breathtaking panoramic view of Venice, its canals, the surrounding
islands and the waters of the lagoon. From here one may survey the
anatomy of the city in all its different parts in a way only otherwise
possible on maps or old engravings. The view is especially impressive

ARSENALE

St Mark's Square

BACINO DI SAN MARCO

❶
SAN GIORGIO MAGGIORE

during one of the historical regattas, when – as in a scene by Cana-letto – the festively decorated gondolas gather in the Bacino di San Marco directly beneath the tower. As an example of the theatre of travel, what a stupendous parting image the poet recommended so warmly to the young bride.

RILKE'S OWN DEPARTURE from Venice was not so poetic. His last two visits after 1912 were marked by dissonance, conflict and disap-pointment. In May 1914 the poet spent four days in the city with the pianist Magda von Hattingberg (better known to Rilke enthusiasts by the name the poet gave her, 'Benvenuta' – 'the Welcomed'). She was one of his great loves – by letter at least. As ever, living together in the real world was difficult. After a disastrous visit to Duino Castle (the princess disliked Magda and had her play the piano for her guests as if she were an employee), the couple split up in Venice. When Rilke went moaning to the princess, she gave him a piece of her mind: 'Dottor Serafico!!! I would really like to give you a blast-ing – I believe you need to be told off properly, like a baby – which is what you are really, as well as a great poet ... Oh Dottor Serafico! *Everyone* is lonely, and *must* remain so, and *must* endure it [...]. And why must you be always trying to save these foolish geese, who ought to be saving themselves – or let the devil take the geese [...] It seems to me, D.S., that the late Don Juan was a choirboy compared to you – And you must always be seeking out these weeping willows, who, believe me, are not actually that unhappy – it is *you, you yourself,* who are reflected in all those eyes –'[172]

RILKE'S LAST STAY in Venice, from 11 June to 13 July 1920, proceeded still more dramatically. At first sight, everything was as before. After a brief period at the Hotel Europe Rilke stayed in the mezzanine, as normal, spent his evenings chattering with the Valmarana ladies and his days roaming about the city. But he had changed, and the city had as well. For the poet, the First World War seemed an 'unholy demolition of what had been'. It is true that he had lived through the conflict working in a military archive in Vienna, outwardly unharmed. But he had scarcely managed to write a word the entire time and the *Duino Elegies* remained in fragments. Rilke foresaw that the break-up of the Habsburg Empire threatened his former life as a poet to the aristocracy. And his age oppressed him. At forty years old, he was no longer the aspiring young poet.

Rilke's keyword for the period was 'rupture'. After the 'rupture' of 1914, he thought that he could in Venice resume the friendship and patronage of the Princess von Thurn und Taxis and his old way of life. He did not succeed. Even the formalities went awry. As an Austrian Rilke had to wrestle with various passport difficulties before he was even allowed to enter the city. And then the prices: 'The enormous sums they extract from you, especially if you are a foreigner, make you realise the poor state of the Lira (example: I bought a shaving brush, because mine had been forgotten –; it cost 50 Lire and was not of the best quality. I have now adopted it as my unit of currency, saying of things: this costs two or three or however many shaving brushes).'[173]

Inflation hurt the long-term residents of the city as well – even the aristocrats, who had never before thought about money, had to do so now. The entire social fabric of Venice had been reordered, as the poet also recognised: 'In spite of having my carefree and fortunate refuge in the *mezzanino*, everything is, to be frank, expensive, compared to how things used to be –, very few Venetians, starting with the Valmaranas, still have their own gondola, because the gondoliers, even if they are permanently employed, require 40 Lire a day, not including their various perks, – they now charge foreigners 10 to 12 francs per hour, which completely prohibits having a gondola wait for you, as in the old days, – everywhere has changed so much, if one looks carefully, on the Piazza, in the old cafés Florian and Quadri, there is no more "society", no genuine old Venetians, at best a couple of gentlemen passing by, it is the same in the evening on the Canal –, a few foreigners, otherwise no one, instead of gondolas there are sailboats, which were once an exceptional sight, in which people, including the gondolieri, having earned enough money during the day, sail about with their families ... There have been no "vaporetti" for eleven days, each day the celebrating workers promenade ostentatiously, calmly strolling around the city. Where did they get the money for such a lengthy strike?'[174]

There were constant strikes – one time it was the postal workers (a catastrophe for a prolific correspondent like Rilke), another time the steamboat crews walked out: 'The vaporetti have been on strike for a week, one might be thankful for their absence, had it not become impossible to obtain a gondola as a result.'[175] Rilke painfully realised that his old way of life in the city had been overtaken: 'For now let me say only that it is impossible for me to piece my life back together as I had intended after the rupture of the pre-war world –, everything has changed, and travel focused on "enjoyment", on a guileless and rather idle receptivity, the travel, in short, of the "educated" traveller, has disappeared forever. In the future it will "become empty", which naturally will not stop many from continuing to pursue it, without registering how used up an enterprise it is. I believe that all aesthetic contemplation that has no direct purpose will henceforth be impossible, – it will be essentially impossible, for example, to "gaze at pictures" in a church [...]. You would not believe, princess, how different, how *different* the world has become, the task now is to understand it.' [176]

For the first time we find Rilke being critical of his aristocratic patrons and the social abyss which ultimately divided him from them: 'And I was aware again of how little the Valmaranas are able to imagine *what* I need; even the Princess T. *cannot do it*, she has a vague idea that on the whole I get by with a minimum for my necessities, but how exactly to define these ten necessities, which ultimately have to be supplied within the limits of this minimum if my existence is to be secure, clear and productive: for this she has neither the insight, the love, nor the patience. These people have for centuries been quite accustomed to presuming that the require-ments of practical existence are ultimately a matter for the domes-tics, with the result that they will always miss the fundamentals of any situation: such things belong to the world and work of one's servants. This explains the in-the-end-not-so-happy feeling in their wonderfully well looked-after houses [...].'[177]

When Eleonora Duse announced she was coming, Rilke took it as a welcome pretext and, on 13 July 1920, fled pell-mell. He never returned to Venice. He found a new adoptive homeland in Switzer-land – and a new motherly friend: not an aristocrat, but an indus-trialist's wife, Nanny Wunderly-Wolkart, a thoroughly solid woman, helpful, caring and practical. Rilke sent her lists of requests, and she arranged everything for him, from envelopes to bed socks. He completed the *Elegies* in 1922 in Muzot. Unusually, he gave them a dedication, to his old friend and patron: 'The Duino Elegies. The Property of Princess Marie von Thurn und Taxis-Hohenlohe.'

RILKE WROTE one of his great Venice poems about San Giorgio Maggiore: 'Venetian Morning' (1908) – a beautiful but difficult poem, which portrays Venice as a city made of endless reflected images. That Venice is made of mirrors is among the commonest of Venetian motifs; it is almost a cliché. But there is something more to discover in Rilke's poem: Venice's town planning. For Rilke, the city holds up a mirror to itself in San Giorgio Maggiore. And this is not just a metaphor; it is a precise description of the role of the island church in the ensemble of the city's great buildings. The main façade of Palladio's church is visible from the Piazzetta and the Doge's Palace. The city government made sure this was so in the seventeenth century, by requiring a monastery in front of the church to be torn down, 'in order that the church should be visible from anywhere on the Piazza or in the Doge's Palace'.[178] The church and its domes were not meant to function in isolation; they were the most vital actors in a planned urban dialogue with the city's other buildings and church domes. It is along these axes of sight or, if you like, in these reflections, that one may for the first time appreciate the unified effect of the city's architecture, always renewing itself every time the viewer shifts position. As in Rilke's poem:

Venetian Morning
Dedicated to Richard Beer-Hoffmann

These princely-pampered windows see forever
what deigns to trouble us occasionally:
the city that perpetually, whenever
a glimpse of sky has met a feel of sea,

will start becoming without ever being.
Each morning must be showing her the selection
of opals she wore yesterday and freeing
from the canals reflection on reflection
and bringing past times to her recollection:
then only she'll comply and be agreeing

as any nymph that gave Zeus welcoming.
Her ear-rings tinkling at her ears, she raises
San Giorgio Maggiore up and gazes
with lazy smile into that lovely thing.[179]

Places to See

ASK A VENETIAN for an address and they will often tell you that there is an issue with house numbers and street names – in this city you cannot really rely upon them. To explain: some places you will not find on your first attempt, some even have two addresses, and single-mindedly 'ticking off' the tourist sights on a carefully worked out route is not only almost impossible, it is also contrary to the character of the city. If you understand that getting lost, searching for things, taking byways and making personal discoveries are part and parcel of your adventure accompanied by *Rilke's Venice*, then you will be in sympathy with the poet too. And do not hesitate to ask for help anywhere in Venice: the Venetians are for the most part friendly and helpful – on the telephone as well.

CHURCHES AND SCUOLE

Ai Gesuati (= Santa Maria del Rosario) *Dorsoduro, Fondamenta delle Zattere ai Gesuati*
This church, which Rilke so loved to sit in, is a favourite amongst Venetians for weddings, because it is so beautifully situated at the water's edge. It makes for excellent wedding photos.

Madonna dell'Orto *Cannaregio, Fondamenta Madonna dell'Orto*
Tintoretto's painting 'Presentazione di Maria al Tempio' (1552–3), which Rilke admired greatly, hangs over the entrance to the Chapel of St Maurus.

Il Redentore *Campo Redentore on La Giudecca*
Rilke was quick to visit this church on the second day of his first visit to Venice in 1897, because Goethe before him had praised it in his *Italian Journey* ('Palladio's great, beautiful work' ... 'The interior of Il Redentore is equally exquisite.' 3 October 1786)

The way to the cloister garden lies to the left of the Church, at the end of Calle dei Frati. At present it is possible to view the garden on request.

San Giorgio Maggiore *Campo San Giorgio on San Giorgio Maggiore island.*
The lift is in the Campanile. The opening times for the church and the tower sometimes differ.

'That lovely thing', as Rilke called it in his poem 'Venetian Morning', is, together with Il Redentore, the only church in Venice to have been designed entirely by Palladio. The master architect, who began work on building the church in 1566, did not however live long enough to see it completed.

San Marco *San Marco, Piazza San Marco*
Whereas most writers have gone into rhapsodies, Goethe wrote barely five lines on the basilica. Only the Quadriga really seemed to interest him: 'I saw the horses on Saint Mark's close up. Looking up at them from below you can easily make out that they are blotchy, partly a beautiful yellow metallic sheen, partly tarnished verdigris. Looking at them from close by, one realises that they were once completely gilded and are now covered in wounds, where the barbarians,

instead of filing off the gold, tried to hack it out. It is good that the shapes survive, at least. They make a splendid team of horses, I would like to hear a real horse expert discussing them.' (*Italian Journey*, 8 October 1786)

Santa Maria Gloriosa dei Frari (= I Frari) *San Polo, Campo dei Frari*
Titian's 'Assunta' ('Assumption of the Virgin') painted in 1518, is here in the choir. Rilke admired it on his first visit to Venice in 1897 and again on his last, in 1920.

Santa Maria della Salute *Dorsoduro, Campo della Salute*
Rilke could see this church by the great Venetian architect Baldassare Longhena (1598–1682), with its famous cupola, from the Princess von Thurn und Taxis's mezzanine.

Santa Maria Formosa *Castello, Campo Santa Maria Formosa*
Rilke was already raving about the 'lovely Santa Maria Formosa church' in 1908. On 3 April 1911 he visited it with the Princess von Thurn und Taxis. The memorial tablets for the Helleman brothers, as mentioned in the first Duino Elegy, frame the south door in the right-hand transept. The inscriptions for the two brothers are located over the doorway; Antonius's tablet is on the right, Gulielmus's on the left.

Scuola Dalmati di S. Giorgio degli Schiavoni *Castello 3259A, Calle dei Furlani*
A Renaissance *gesamtkunstwerk*, preserved almost in its entirety, with Carpaccio's painted histories of Saints Jerome, Triphon and George.

TIP: As a rule you will have to pay for entry to Venice's churches. If you are visiting a number of the churches mentioned here, it is cheaper to use the 'Chorus Pass'. The Pass is valid for a year and can be purchased at any of the participating churches.

MUSEUMS AND GALLERIES

Ca' d'Oro, Galleria Franchetti *Cannaregio 3932, Calle di Ca' d'Oro*
Rilke admired the skill of the then recent renovation of this palace. It has now, however, fallen back into disrepair. It boasts magnificent views out onto the Grand Canal and the Palazzi opposite.

Ca Rezzonico, Museo del Settecento Veneziano *(Museum of Eighteenth-Century Venice) Dorsoduro 3136, Fondamenta Rezzonico*
Rilke visited this palace in 1903 on the trail of the English poet Robert Browning, who had died here on 12 December 1889 in the rooms under the roof. There is nothing here now to recall the poet, however, and the collected of Venetian paintings on display is undistinguished. Nevertheless, you ought definitely to climb up to the higher storeys, in order to experience a typical Venetian mezzanine, like the apartment of the Princess von Thurn und Taxis.

Gallerie dell'Accademia *Dorsoduro 1050, Campo della Carità*
From his first visit in 1897 Rilke remembered particularly the 'noble plainness' of the building, rather less about the paintings. He went on to visit the Accademia many times. Titian's 'The Presentation of the Virgin at the Temple' (1534–8) in room 24 of the gallery inspired a poem on Mary's life.

Museo Correr *San Marco 52, Piazza San Marco, Procuratie Nuove*
Carpaccio's 1495 masterpiece 'Two Venetian Ladies' (formerly 'The Courtesans') is on the second floor.

Palazzo Ducale *San Marco 1, Piazetta San Marco*
The rooms used by the secret police, their informers and 'spies'
(Rilke in 'A Doge') can only be visited on a guided tour. Book at
least two days in advance.

**Palazzo Mocenigo, Centro Studi di Storia del Tessuto e
Costume** *(Museum of textiles and costume) Santa Croce 1992*
The striking row of ancestral portraits showing this one family's
seven Doges can be found in the *portego* (entrance hall).

Pinacoteca Querini-Stampalia *Castello 5252, Campo S. Maria Formosa*
Mediocre art offering, nevertheless, as Rilke found, a good insight
into Venetian everyday life in an authentic ambience.

TIP: For information on discounted combination tickets, museum
passes and opening hours, visit www.museiciviciveneziani.it

PALACES

Ca' Giustinian
Today home of the Biennale, formerly the luxurious Hotel de
l'Europe. One of Princess von Thurn und Taxis's last memories
of Rilke in Venice was formed here: 'At the end of May 1920 my
husband and I met up [in Venice], Rilke followed a little later and
disembarked at the Hotel Europe, whence I fetched him. I can still
see him, standing on the small flight of steps on the Grand Canal,
laughing as he waved at our gondola.'

Casetta Rossa *(also Casetta delle Rose)*
A small palace on the Grand Canal, somewhat set back from the
water, diagonally opposite the Campo San Vio. Following his first
visit on 4 April 1911, Rilke often spent time here as the guest of

Prince Fritz von Hohenlohe. The Prince's wife, Donna Zina (Mrs von Waldenburg) looked after the keys for the mezzanine. In 1915 the Prince rented out Casetta Rossa to Gabriele d'Annunzio. He lived here when his liaison with Eleonora Duse was long in the past (and not at the same time as she was staying in the Palazzo Barbaro-Wolkoff diagonally opposite, as is often said).

Palazzo Barbaro-Wolkoff

Best seen from the Grand Canal, this palazzo stands between Santa Maria della Salute and Palazzo Venier dei Leoni (today the home of the Guggenheim collection). Eleonora Duse lived here for several years: 'I have installed myself in a small apartment on the top floor of an old palazzo, under the roof, with a large lancet window commanding a view right over the whole city.' Rilke could have rented a room here in later years from Alexander Wolkoff-Mouromtzoff, but he preferred the Princess's mezzanine. The French poet Henri de Régnier lived and worked in the **Palazzo Dario** next door. Rilke would bump into him from time to time while out walking on the Zattere. He particularly admired his French fellow-poet for his outstanding contribution to the rediscovery of the Venetian garden.

Palazzo Barbarigo della Terrazza

On the Grand Canal, by the entrance to Rio San Polo, is the marble terrace where Rilke stood in November 1907. The Palazzo was once famous for its collection of paintings, many of which were sold in bulk to Tsar Nicholas I in 1850. Today the building houses the German Study Centre in Venice.

Palazzo Bembo

On the Grand Canal, not far from the Rialto Bridge. Reputed to have been the residence of the Renaissance philosopher and poet Pietro Bembo, Venice's official city chronicler. The Jew Amedeo

Grassini (father of Margherita Sarfatti, later Mussolini's mistress) bought the famous palace in 1894 and moved in with his family. Rilke got his roses from the 'old garden at Palazzo Bembo' of Princess Titi (=Pauline) von Thurn und Taxis.

Palazzo Cini (formerly Valmarana)   *Dorsoduro 864, Campo San Vio*
This palazzo houses the Vittorio Cini art collection and hosts special exhibitions.

Palazzo Labia   *Cannaregio, Fondamenta Labia*
Viewing of the Sala del Tiepolo by appointment only.

Palazzo Mocenigo and Ca' Mocenigo Vecchia   *On the Grand Canal, opposite San Tomà pier*
Giordano Bruno spent time in the Ca' Mocenigo Vecchia while visiting in 1591–2, before being denounced to the Inquisition by his host Giovanni Mocenigo. Later guests fared rather better with the old-established family: Byron managed to write early parts of *Don Juan* in the Palazzo Mocenigo in 1818–19. Rilke was a frequent guest at the exclusive salon of the beautiful Countess Mocenigo over the summer of 1912.

HOTELS

Bauer   *San Marco 1459, Campo San Moisè*
This traditional hotel, called Hotel D'Italie-Bauer (Grünwald) in Rilke's time, was, according to the 1902 edition of Baedeker, a favourite among German visitors and 'rather less sophisticated'. It was in those days better known for its Austrian cooking. It has reinvented itself since, and today belongs amongst the best five-star hotels in the world. Its cooking is now international.

Danieli   *Castello 4196, Riva degli Schiavoni*
Around the turn of the twentieth century, this was Baedeker's top-ranked hotel. D'Annunzio was staying here when he first met Eleonora Duse. Rilke, being not quite as profligate as his esteemed Italian fellow poet, never had a room here. Today it is still one of the best luxury hotels. The piano bar is open to non-residents as well.

Des Bains   *Lungomare Marconi 17, Lido di Venezia*
Rilke found the luxury hotels on the Lido 'exorbitant stupid buildings' – in spite of his normal enthusiasm for glittering hotels. Thomas Mann stayed here in the summer of 1911; it later served as a location for Lucchino Visconti's film version of *Death in Venice*.

Europa e Regina Grandhotel   *San Marco 2159, Calle Larga XXII Marzo*
Formerly the Hotel Britannia, this is where Rilke stayed on his first visit to Venice, in 1897.

Luna Hotel Baglioni   *San Marco 1243*
A building with a long history: in 1118, when it was a cloister, the Knights Templar lodged here before they travelled on to Jerusalem. In 1574 the building became the guesthouse Locanda della Luna. Rilke stayed here from 29 March to 5 April 1911. Today it offers five-star luxury.

Pensione La Calcina   *Dorsoduro 780, Fondamenta Zattere ai Gesuati*
Old-established *pensione* on Venice's most beautiful promenade. John Ruskin was a long-term guest. The hotel uses as part of its marketing the fact that Rilke wrote letters from here. The private room that the poet rented in early summer 1912 was in fact just around the corner, in what is today Calle del Pistor 775, Campo della Calcina.

BÀCARIS, CAFÉS, RESTAURANTS

Do Mori   *429 San Polo, Calle Do Mori*

Narrow, noisy and packed: at the Do Mori, you eat standing up. No place for a thin-skinned poet, but rightly one of the most famous of Venice's old Bàcari: the 'Francobolli' ('stamps'), as the sandwiches here are called, are outstanding and the prosecco, exclusively produced for Do Mori, is delivered fresh every week from Valdobiaddene.

L'Altanella   *Giudecca 268, Calle delle Erbe*

A family business for four generations. In summer you may sit outside on the terrace adjoining a quiet side-canal, instead of in the small dining room.

Antica Locanda Montin   *Dorsoduro, Fondamenta Eremite 1147 (in some maps and guidebooks: Fondamenta Borgo)*

A restaurant behind San Trovaso, very near to Palazzo Cini and the Accademia. In Rilke's time it offered rustic fare: its bohemian guests nourished themselves on bread, salami and wine. Nowadays the menu is more sophisticated. The pergola in the garden still provides lovely shade.

Caffè Florian   *San Marco 56, Piazza San Marco*

Since 1720 a meeting place of artists and writers, including Lord Byron, Rousseau, George Sand, Alfred de Musset and Schopenhauer. In the summer of 1912 Rilke often came here to chat with his aristocratic friends. On very hot days, while the others drank 'deceptive iced drinks' to cool off, Rilke tried to 'achieve momentary equilibrium with an occasional cup of very hot tea'.

Gran Caffè Quadri *San Marco 120, Piazza San Marco*

Founded under another name in 1638, this is one of Venice's oldest coffeehouses. Here, in 1725, Venetians were able to try Turkish mocha for the first time. The commercial rivalry between Quadri and Florian was of no concern to foreign artists. Henry James, for example, used to eat an ample breakfast at Florian and then have lunch at Quadri. 'True' Venetians, however, preferred to meet at Florian after Caffè Quadri became the favourite of the Austrian occupying forces. Whether this had any effect on Rilke – whose dislike for all things Austrian is well known – is not clear. But in 1920 he regretted the absence of those members of high society whom he had been used to meet here before the First World War.

Taverna La Fenice *San Marco 1939, Campiello della Fenice*

Only a few dishes on the fancy menu – such as *Pasta e fagioli* (pasta with beans) – recall the 'authentic Venetian' atmosphere, in which the Princess von Thurn und Taxis and Rilke had breakfast in 1920. In those days this inn, which dates back to the latter end of the eighteenth century, was a typical working man's taverna, serving wine and hefty meals.

SQUARES, STREETS AND OTHER SIGHTS

Arsenal *Castello*

The Arsenal is still guarded as it was in *La Serenissima*'s glory days. The two lions that watch over the imposing entrance gate were looted from Greece in 1687 by Francesco Morosini, the last Doge to serve at the same time as overall commander of the fleet. His many victories (against the Turks among others) were not however enough to halt the decline of both the city and its shipyard.

Campo del Ghetto Nuovo
The Museo Ebraico e Sinagoghe, Cannaregio 2902/b offers guided tours of the Ghetto, including its more recent history. Available in Italian and English.

Campo San Polo *San Polo*
Venice's second largest square is surprisingly contemplative and green: a small tree-lined oasis in the city of water. Formerly the setting for popular festivals, bull-baiting and al fresco religious services, it today plays host to a Carnival shindig in February and an open-air cinema over the summer. At other times, it is full of day-to-day Venetian life.

Campo Santa Maria Formosa *Castello*
As so often in Venice, leaving the main tourist sights behind you has its rewards. This square is no distance from Piazza San Marco, but your Campari will cost only a third as much.

Campo San Trovaso and the gondola boatyard *Dorsoduro*
With its ancient wooden sheds, the gondola boatyard resembles an alpine village in the middle of the city of marble. In 1934 Max Reinhardt used the Campo as the backdrop to an open-air performance of *The Merchant of Venice*.

Campo San Vio
No longer noisy as it was in Rilke's time. On the contrary: a quiet, small square with views of the Grand Canal and Palazzo Cini formerly Valmarana.

Cimitero ebraico *Via Cipro 70, Lido di Venezia*
Goethe wrote of his visit to the cemetery on the Lido: 'On the Lido, not far from the sea, Englishmen lie buried, and further on, Jews,

neither of whom could be laid to rest in hallowed ground. I found the grave of the noble Consul Smith and his first wife. I owe him for my copy of Palladio and so thanked him for it at his unhallowed grave. And the grave is not only unhallowed, but also half covered over.' (8 October 1786)

Today you may only visit the Jewish graveyard with a guide. Tours are available irregularly, in Italian and English and not in winter. If you are interested, call the Museo Ebraico, where you will receive a very friendly welcome.

Pescheria and Erberia *San Polo*

There has been a fish market in operation here for a thousand years. If you want to watch the unloading of the produce (still a worthwhile experience), you will need to get up very early. All the displays are laid out by 08.30 at the latest and are packed away again by noon.

Spadaria *San Marco, between Calle Larga San Marco and Campo San Giuliano, behind St Mark's Square*

Rilke wished to have a fan, like one he had seen at Contessina Pia's, 'painstakingly assembled' in a craftsman's workshop here. There was only one problem: the high price. The work was going to cost 40 Francs. Today the poet would have had a different problem: scarcely any of the traditional souvenirs which are sold in the streets around St Mark's Square, be they fans, lace or glassware, are still produced in Venice. Most of the fans come from Spain; half of all the 'Murano' glass being sold is manufactured in Taiwan; and almost the only place to find the renowned Burano lace any more is in a museum. None of the lace doilies that are on sale in approximately 130 shops and stalls around Venice are any more woven on the islands of Venice, according to Girolamo Marcello, president of the 'Foundation for the Preservation of Burano Lace', at any rate. The real thing is nowadays only available at extraordinary cost.

Zattere

This waterside pavement is so long that it changes its name several times: from Fondamenta Zattere Ponte Lungo, where you will find Luigi Nono's birthplace and the former Pension Romanelli, along with numerous restaurants and ice cream parlours; via Fondamenta Zattere ai Gesuati, with the church of the same name; and Fondamenta Zattere allo Spirito Santo, where the poet Ezra Pound, who lived nearby at Calle Querini 252, used to like to stroll; to Fondamenta Zattere ai Saloni, with its boatyards, canoeing clubs and the Magazzini del Sale (the old salt stores), leading up to the customs house, the Dogana da Mar.

GARDENS

For general information contact the Wigwam Club Giardini Storici Veneziana (*www.giardini-venezia.it*), which organises tours of Venice's gardens, for small groups if required, though mostly in Italian.

Giardini Papadopoli *Santa Croce, Piazzale Roma*

'Whatever happens, you must see the lovely Giardini Papadopoli near Palazzo Labia; get permission at the old Palazzo Tiepolo-Papodopoli, which belongs to the antiques dealer Mr Guggenheim.' Rilke's advice to Gisela von der Heydt is only half true today. Along with the Giardini Publicci (the base of the Biennale) and the Royal Garden, the Giardini Papadopoli remains one of the few substantial gardens in Venice that is permanently open to the public. But it has lost much of its charm, indeed seems now rather run down. There is little to recall its atmosphere in the nineteenth century, when the stage designer at La Fenice Theatre, Francesco Bagnara, first laid it out in the English romantic style. The many exotic plants and the famous terrace with its view over the Grand Canal are later embellishments.

Giardino Eden *Giudecca, at the far end of Rio della Croce*
'It is drawn up into space like the Paradise on the frescoes in Pisa: the limit of what we may yet think of as earthly; the place where the earthly, as if it were dying away, is perpetually overflowing into the heavens, rising up, fleeing from us.' Today the 'Garden of Eden', which Rilke recommended so enthusiastically to Gisela von der Heydt, is bordered in a very earthly way by canals, brick walls and locked gates.

Notes

WORKS FREQUENTLY REFERRED to have been given abbreviated titles: all these are listed in the 'Further Reading'. Other works' titles are abbreviated after their first appearance.

All of Rilke's poems are quoted in the translations of J B Leishman. All prose quotations have been freshly translated for this edition, but where an English version already exists, that is referenced here in preference to the German original.

1. Zweig, *World of Yesterday*, pp 114–15.
2. *Selected Letters*, p 420 (to K X Kappus, 29 October 1903).
3. Rainer Maria Rilke, *Briefe*, from the Rilke Archive in Weimar ed by Karl Altheim (Frankfurt am Main: 1975) Vol 1, p 172 (to Clara Rilke, 11 October 1907).
4. Rilke, *Notebooks of Malte Laurids Brigge* , p 26.
5. Rainer Maria Rilke, *Briefwechsel mit Anton Kippenberg 1906 bis 1926* (Frankfurt am Main/Leipzig: 1995) Vol 1, p 341 (to Anton Kippenberg, 13 May 1912).
6. Rudolf Kassner, *Rilke: Gesammelte Erinnerungen 1926–1956* (Pfullingen: 1976) p 30.
7. Zweig, *World of Yesterday*, p 117.
8. Rainer Maria Rilke and Marie von Thurn und Taxis, *Briefwechsel* (Frankfurt am Main: 1986) Vol 1, p 133 (5 April 1912).

9. Cited in Helmut Woche, *Rilke und Italien* (Gießen: 1940) p 73.

10. von Thurn und Taxis, *Memoirs*, p 132.

11. von Thurn und Taxis, *Memoirs*, p 204.

12. von Thurn und Taxis, *Memoirs*, p 134.

13. Rainer Maria Rilke, *Die Briefe an Karl und Elizabeth von der Heydt 1905–1922* (Frankfurt am Main: 1986) p 147 (to Gisela von der Heydt, 24 March 1908).

14. von Thurn und Taxis, *Memoirs*, p 147.

15. von Thurn und Taxis, *Memoirs*, p 177.

16. Rainer Maria Rilke, *Briefe aus Muzot* (Leipzig: 1937) p 409 (17 March 1926).

17. Rilke, *Briefe*, ed by Karl Altheim, p 183 (to Clara Rilke, 11 October 1907).

18. Kassner, *Rilke*, p 15.

19. Cited in Joachim W Storck, 'Rilkes frühestes Venedig-Erlebnis', pp 19 to 32 in *Blätter der Rilke-Gesellschaft*, Heft 16/17 (1989/90), p 22 (to Nora Goudstikker, 25 March 1897).

20. Rilke, *Briefe an Karl und Elizabeth von der Heydt*, p 144 (to Gisela von der Heydt, 24 March 1908).

21. Rainer Maria Rilke, *Das Florenzer Tagebuch* (Frankfurt am Main/Leipzig: 1994) pp 25f.

22. Rainer Maria Rilke, *Briefe an Sidonie Nádherny von Borutin* (Frankfurt am Main: 1973) p 47 (19 November 1907).

23. Rilke, *Briefe an Sidonie Nádherny von Borutin*, p 48.

24. Rilke, *Briefe*, ed by Karl Altheim, p 214 (to Clara Rilke, 20 November 1907).

25. Cited in Freedman, *Life*, p 281 (letter of 26 November 1907).

26. Cited in Freedman, *Life*, p 281 (letter of 1 December 1907).

27. Rainer Maria Rilke, *Briefe an Nanny Wunderly-Volkart* (Frankfurt am Main: 1977) Vol 1, pp 261f (5 July 1920).

28. Rilke, *Notebooks of Malte Laurids Brigge* , p 119.

29. Rilke, *Duino Elegies*, p 27.
30. Cited in Freedman, p 282 (letter of 7 December 1907).
31. Cited in Gunnar Decker, *Rilkes Frauen oder die Erfindung der Liebe* (Leipzig: 2004) p 143.
32. Rilke, *Briefe an Sidonie Nádherny von Borutin*, p 155 (7 June 1912)
33. Rilke, *Briefwechsel mit Marie von Thurn und Taxis* (Frankfurt am Main: 1986) Vol I, p 157 (22 May 1912) and Rilke, *Briefe an Sidonie Nádherny von Borutin*, p 155 (7 June 1912).
34. Rilke, *Briefwechsel mit Marie von Thurn und Taxis*, Vol I, p 149 (14 May 1912).
35. Rilke, *Briefwechsel mit Marie von Thurn und Taxis*, Vol I, p 155 (18 May 1912).
36. Rilke, *Briefwechsel mit Marie von Thurn und Taxis*, Vol I, p 143 (9 May 1912).
37. Rilke, *Briefwechsel mit Marie von Thurn und Taxis*, Vol I, p 149 (14 May 1912).
38. von Thurn und Taxis, *Memoirs*, p 171.
39. Cited in Rätus Luck, '"Mezzanino": Rainer Maria Rilke und die Damen Valmarana' pp 43 to 55 in *Blätter der Rilke-Gesellschaft*, Heft 16/17 (1989/90) pp 43f.
40. Rilke, *Selected Letters*, p 301 (25 June 1920).
41. Letters/von Thurn und Taxis, p 45.
42. von Thurn und Taxis, *Memoirs*, p 171.
43. Letters/von Thurn und Taxis, p 46.
44. Zweig, *World of Yesterday*, p 117.
45. Letters/Benvenuta, p 60.
46. Rilke, *Briefwechsel mit Marie von Thurn und Taxis*, Vol I, p 174 (6 July 1912).
47. Rilke, *Briefwechsel mit Marie von Thurn und Taxis*, Vol I, p 160 (28 May 1912).

48. Rilke, *Briefe an Nanny Wunderly-Volkart*, Vol 1, p 255 (22 June 1920).

49. Letters/von Thurn und Taxis, pp 45–6.

50. Zweig, *World of Yesterday*, p 117.

51. Rilke, *Briefe an Nanny Wunderly-Volkart*, Vol 1, p 263 (6 July 1920).

52. Letters/Benvenuta, p 60.

53. Rilke, *Briefe an Nanny Wunderly-Volkart*, Vol 1, p 262 (5 July 1920).

54. Rilke, *Briefe an Nanny Wunderly-Volkart*, Vol 1, p 256 (22 June 1920).

55. Letters/Andreas-Salomé, p 200.

56. *Selected Letters*, pp 301–2 (25 June 1920).

57. Rilke, *Briefwechsel mit Marie von Thurn und Taxis*, Vol 1, p 155 (18 May 1912).

58. Zweig, *World of Yesterday*, p 115.

59. See Freedman, *Life*, p 206.

60. von Thurn und Taxis, *Memoirs*, p 161.

61. Letters/von Thurn und Taxis, p 25 (15 December 1911).

62. Rainer Maria Rilke, *Briefe an Schweizer Freunde* (Frankfurt am Main/Leipzig: 1994) p 93 (to Dory von der Mühll, 1 July 1920).

63. Rilke, *Briefwechsel mit Marie von Thurn und Taxis*, Vol 2, p 605 (23 June 1920).

64. Cited in Storck, 'Rilkes frühestes Venedig-Erlebnis', p 25 (to Nora Goudstikker, 28 March 1897).

65. Letters/Andreas-Salomé, p 118.

66. Rilke, *Florenzer Tagebuch*, p 25.

67. Rilke, *Briefe*, ed by Karl Altheim, p 174 (to Clara Rilke, 7 October 1907).

68. Rilke, *Briefe an Karl und Elizabeth von der Heydt*, pp 147–9 (to Gisela von der Heydt, 24 March 1908).

69. Rilke, *Briefwechsel mit Marie von Thurn und Taxis*, Vol 1, p 149 (14 May 1912).

70. Cited in Storck, 'Rilkes frühestes Venedig-Erlebnis', p 23 (to Nora Goudstikker, 27 March 1897).

71. Rilke, *Briefe an Karl und Elizabeth von der Heydt*, p 147 (to Gisela von der Heydt, 24 March 1908).

72. Rilke, *Briefwechsel mit Marie von Thurn und Taxis*, Vol 1, pp 128f (22 March 1912).

73. Rilke, *Briefe an Nanny Wunderly-Volkart*, Vol 1, p 262 (5 July 1920).

74. Cited in Storck, 'Rilkes frühestes Venedig-Erlebnis', p 24 (to Nora Goudstikker, 28 March 1897).

75. Rilke, *New Poems*, p 247.

76. Zweig, *World of Yesterday*, p 113.

77. Eckart Peterich, *Italien: Ein Führer. Erster Band: Oberitalien, Toskana, Umbrien* (München: 1985) pp 124f.

78. Rilke, *Briefe an Karl und Elizabeth von der Heydt*, p 147 (to Gisela von der Heydt, 24 March 1908).

79. Rilke, *Briefe an Schweizer Freunde*, p 89 (to Dory Von der Mühll, 22 June 1920).

80. Rilke, *New Poems*, p 247.

81. Rilke, *New Poems*, p 119.

82. Rilke, *New Poems*, p 245.

83. Rilke, *Briefe an Sidonie Nádherny von Borutin*, p 49 (24 November 1907).

84. Letters/von Thurn und Taxis, p 7 (29 April 1910).

85. Rilke, *Briefe an Sidonie Nádherny von Borutin*, p 147 (8 March 1912).

86. Rilke, *Briefwechsel mit Marie von Thurn und Taxis*, Vol 1, p 121 (2 March 1912).

87. Dante, *The Portable Dante*, tr and ed by Mark Musa (Penguin: 1995) p 112.

88. Rilke, *Notebooks of Malte Laurids Brigge*, p 26.

89. Rilke, *Stories of God*, p 69.

90. von Thurn und Taxis, *Memoirs*, p 142.

91. Rilke, *Duino Elegies*, p 29.

92. Cited in Ulrich Fülleborn/Manfred Engel (eds), *Rilkes 'Duineser Elegien'* (Frankfurt am Main: 1982) Vol 2, pp 189f. The Latin text is reproduced on page 207.

93. Johann Wolfgang Goethe, *Tagebuch der Italienischen Reise 1786* (Frankfurt am Main: 1976) pp 100f.

94. Rilke, *Stories of God*, p 68.

95. Rilke, *Stories of God*, p 68.

96. Rainer Maria Rilke/Mathilde Vollmoeller, *Briefwechsel 1906 bis 1914* (Frankfurt am Main/Leipzig: 1993) p 133 (11 February 1912).

97. Rilke, *Briefe an Karl und Elizabeth von der Heydt*, p 151 (to Gisela von der Heydt, 24 March 1908).

98. Rilke, *Stories of God*, p 69.

99. von Thurn und Taxis, *Memoirs*, p 159.

100. Rilke, *Stories of God*, p 69.

101. Attilio Milano, *Storia degli ebrei in Italia* (Torino: 1992) p 521.

102. Rilke, *Stories of God*, p 71.

103. Rilke, *Stories of God*, p 71.

104. Rilke, *Stories of God*, p 71.

105. Richard Sennett, *Flesh and Stone: The Body and the City in Western Civilisation* (London and Boston: 1994) p 216.

106. Rilke, *Stories of God*, p 70.

107. Rilke, *Stories of God*, p 71.

108. William Shakespeare, *The Merchant of Venice*, ed by M M Mahood (Cambridge: 1987) p 77 (Act I, Scene iii).

109. Shakespeare, *The Merchant of Venice*, p 110 (Act III, Scene i).

110. Cited in Sennett, *Flesh and Stone*, p 242.

111. Rilke, *Stories of God*, p 72.

112. Rudolf Kassner, 'Zum Briefwechsel zwischen R. M. Rilke und der Fürstin Marie von Thurn und Taxis-Hohenlohe', pp XIII to XXXVII in *Briefwechsel mit Marie von Thurn und Taxis*, Vol 1, here p XXXI.

113. Rilke, *Briefwechsel mit Marie von Thurn und Taxis*, Vol 1, p 163 (5 June 1912).

114. Rilke, *Poems* (ed Peter Washington), pp 106–7.

115. Cited in Manfred Engel (ed), *Rilke-Handbuh: Leben – Wirk – Wirkung* (Stuttgart: 2004) p 356 (to Princess Sizzo, 6 January 1922).

116. Rilke, *Briefe an Schweizer Freunde*, p 89 (to Dory von der Mühll, 22 June 1920).

117. Cited in Storck, 'Rilkes frühestes Venedig-Erlebnis', p 23 (to Nora Goudstikker, 27 March 1897).

118. Cited in Storck, 'Rilkes frühestes Venedig-Erlebnis', p 24 (to Nora Goudstikker, 28 March 1897).

119. Cited in Storck, 'Rilkes frühestes Venedig-Erlebnis', p 24 (to Nora Goudstikker, 28 March 1897).

120. Rilke, *Selected Letters*, p 304 (25 June 1920).

121. Rilke, *Briefe an Schweizer Freunde*, p 93 (to Dory von der Mühll, 1 July 1920).

122. Rilke, *Briefe an Schweizer Freunde*, p 90 (to Dory von der Mühll, 1 July 1920).

123. Rainer Maria Rilke, *Briefe aus den Jahren 1907–1914*, Leipzig 1933, pp 26f (to Clara Rilke, 22 November 1907).

124. Rilke, *Notebooks of Malte Laurids Brigge*, pp 203–5.

125. von Thurn und Taxis, *Memoirs*, p 172.

126. Rilke, *Briefwechsel mit Marie von Thurn und Taxis*, Vol 1, p 148 (14 May 1912).

127. Rilke, *Briefe an Nanny Wunderly-Volkart*, Vol 1, p 263 (6 July 1920).

128. Rilke, *Briefwechsel mit Marie von Thurn und Taxis*, Vol 1, p 147 (14 May 1912).

129. Letters/von Thurn und Taxis, p 45 (18 May 1912).

130. Kassner, *Rilke*, p 86.

131. Rilke, *Briefwechsel mit Marie von Thurn und Taxis*, Vol 1, p 157 (22 May 1912).

132. von Thurn und Taxis, *Memoirs*, p 171.

133. Cited in Ilsedore B Jonas, *Rilke und die Duse* (Frankfurt am Main/Leipzig: 1993) p 93 (to Helene von Nostitz, 16 July 1912).

134. Cited in Maria Gazzetti, *Gabriele d'Annunzio* (Reinbek b. Hamburg: 2000) p 63.

135. Letters/von Thurn und Taxis, p 48 (12 July 1912).

136. Letters/von Thurn und Taxis, p 51 (20 July 1912).

137. von Thurn und Taxis, *Memoirs*, p 172.

138. Letters/von Thurn und Taxis, p 51 (20 July 1912).

139. Letters/Benvenuta, p 60.

140. Letters/von Thurn und Taxis, p 49 (12 July 1912).

141. Letters/von Thurn und Taxis, pp 48–9 (12 July 1912).

142. von Thurn und Taxis, *Memoirs*, p 175.

143. Letters/von Thurn und Taxis, p 57 (3 August 1912).

144. Letters/von Thurn und Taxis, p 52 (20 July 1912).

145. Letters/von Thurn und Taxis, p 60 (26 August 1912) and Letters/von Thurn und Taxis, p 59 (8 August 1912).

146. Cited in Jonas, *Rilke und die Duse*, p 123 (to Helene von Nostitz, 17 July 1914).

147. Letters/Andreas-Salomé, p 315.

148. von Thurn und Taxis, *Memoirs*, p 157.

149. Rilke, *Briefe an Karl und Elizabeth von der Heydt*, p 149 (to Gisela von der Heydt, 24 March 1908).

150. Rilke, *Briefe an Nanny Wunderly-Volkart*, Vol 1, p 256 (22 June 1920).

151. Rilke, *Briefe an Nanny Wunderly-Volkart*, Vol 1, p 257 (22 June 1920).

152. Letters/von Thurn und Taxis, p 39 (29 March 1912).

153. J W Goethe, *Italian Journey 1786–1788*, tr W H Auden and Elizabeth Mayer (Harmondsworth: 1970) p 96.

154. Rilke, *Briefe an Sidonie Nádherny von Borutin*, pp 153f (10 April 1912).

155. Rilke, *Briefwechsel mit Marie von Thurn und Taxis*, Vol 1, p 153 (18 May 1912).

156. Rilke, *Briefwechsel mit Marie von Thurn und Taxis*, Vol 1, p 139 (9 April 1912).

157. Rilke, *Briefwechsel mit Marie von Thurn und Taxis*, Vol 2, p 606 (28 June 1920).

158. Thomas Mann, *Death in Venice and Other Stories*, tr David Luke (London: 1998) p 223.

159. Rainer Maria Rilke, *Briefe an das Ehepaar S. Fischer* (Zürich: 1947) p 70 (to Hedwig Fischer, 6 November 1912).

160. Rainer Maria Rilke, *Briefe an das Ehepaar S. Fischer* (Zürich: 1947) pp 72f (to Hedwig Fischer, 31 December 1912).

161. Marlene Dietrich, *My Life*, tr Salvator Attanasio (London: 1989) p 133.

162. Rilke, *Briefe an Nanny Wunderly-Volkart*, Vol 1, p 253 (21 June 1920).

163. Rilke, *Briefe an Nanny Wunderly-Volkart*, Vol 1, pp 258f (1 July 1920).

164. Rilke, *Briefwechsel mit Marie von Thurn und Taxis*, Vol 1, p 133 (5 April 1912).

165. Cited in Storck, 'Rilkes frühestes Venedig-Erlebnis', p 25 (to Nora Goudstikker, 28 March 1897).

166. Letters/Nölke, p 39.

167. Rainer Maria Rilke/Ellen Key, *Briefwechsel* (Frankfurt am Main/Leipzig: 1993) pp 37f (18 August 1903).

168. Rilke/Key, *Briefwechsel*, p 38 (20 August 1903).

169. Rilke/Key, *Briefwechsel*, p 39 (3 November 1903).

170. Rilke, *Briefe an Sidonie Nádherny von Borutin*, p 51 (25 November 1907).

171. Rilke, *Briefe an Karl und Elizabeth von der Heydt*, p 150 (to Gisela von der Heydt, 24 March 1908).

172. Letters/von Thurn und Taxis, pp 133–4.

173. Rilke, *Briefe an Nanny Wunderly-Volkart*, Vol 1, p 254 (21 June 1920).

174. Rilke, *Briefe an Schweizer Freunde*, pp 91f (to Dory von der Mühll, 1 July 1920)

175. Rilke, *Selected Letters*, p 303 (26 June 1920).

176. Letters/von Thurn und Taxis, p 188 (23 July 1920).

177. Rilke, *Briefe an Nanny Wunderly-Volkart*, Vol 1, pp 432f (20 May 1920).

178. Cited in Norbert Huse, *Venedig: Von der Kunst, eine Stadt im Wasser zu bauen* (München: 2005) p 139.

179. Rilke, *New Poems*, pp 243–5.

Further Reading

THE CHALLENGES of Rilke's major poetic works have attracted translators in great numbers. J B Leishman, one of Rilke's earliest translators into English, remains one of the best. As he has also translated more of Rilke's poems – including those about Venice – than anyone else, we have used his translations of the poems here. All prose quotations have been freshly translated for this edition. The work of Stephen Mitchell offers a good and more recent alternative to Leishman while William Gass's *Reading Rilke* offers a passionate and witty survey of Rilke translation – and an exploration of translation in general.

This bibliography refers the reader only to work in the English language. Bibliographies of the German originals, and lengthier guides to reading, can be found in Ralph Freedman's biography of the poet.

Abbreviations used in the footnotes are given here in square brackets.

Poetry

Requiem and Other Poems, tr J B Leishman (2nd Enlarged Edn, The Hogarth Press, London: 1949).

Poems 1906 to 1926, tr J B Leishman (The Hogarth Press, London: 1957).

New Poems, tr J B Leishman (The Hogarth Press, London: 1964).

Sonnets to Orpheus, tr J B Leishman (The Hogarth Press, London: 1936).

Duino Elegies, tr J B Leishman and Stephen Spender (3rd edn, revised, The Hogarth Press, London: 1948).

Later Poems, tr J B Leishman (Hogarth Press, London: 1938).

Poems, various translators, ed Peter Washington (Everyman's Library, London: 1996).

The Selected Poetry of Rainer Maria Rilke, ed and tr Stephen Mitchell (Pan, London: 1987)

Prose

Stories of God, tr M D Herder Norton (Norton, New York: 1932; original German publication 1900) [Rilke, *Stories of God*].

The Notebooks of Malte Laurids Brigge, tr M D Herder Norton (Norton, New York: 1949, reissued 1992; original German publication 1910) [Rilke, *Notebooks of Malte Laurids Brigge*].

Correspondence

Rainer Maria Rilke: Selected Letters 1902–1926, tr R F C Hull, introduced by John Bayley (Quartet Books, London and New York: 1988; original English edition published by Macmillan in 1946 and 1945 [*Letters to a Young Poet*], original German editions, Insel Verlag 1935 and 1929) [*Selected Letters*].

Rainer Maria Rilke and Lou Andreas-Salomé: The Correspondence, tr Edward Snow and Michael Winkler (W W Norton and Company, New York and London: 2006; originally published in German by Insel Verlag, Frankfurt am Main, ed Ernst Pfeiffer) [Letters/Andreas-Salomé].

Rilke and Benvenuta: An Intimate Correspondence, ed Magda von
Hattingberg (Benvenuta), tr Joel Agee (Fromm International
Publishing Corporation, New York: 1987; originally published
as *Briefwechsel mit Benvenuta*: 1954) [Letters/Benvenuta]
Letters to Merline: 1919–1922, tr Violet M Macdonald (Methuen,
London: 1951). [Letters/Merline]
Correspondence in Verse with Erika Mitterer, Rainer Maria Rilke,
tr N K Cruickshank (The Hogarth Press, London: 1953; first
published in German in 1950) [Letters/Mitterer].
Letters to Frau Gudi Nölke during his life in Switzerland, ed Paul
Obermüller, tr Violet M Macdonald (The Hogarth Press,
London: 1955) [Letters/Nölke].
*The Letters of Rainer Maria Rilke and Princess Marie von Thurn
und Taxis*, tr Nora Wydenbruck (The Hogarth Press, London:
1958; originally published by Max Niehans Verlag, Zürich: 1951)
[Letters/von Thurn und Taxis].

Other works

Belmore, H W, *Rilke's craftsmanship: an analysis of his poetic style*
(Oxford: 1954).
Dietrich, Marlene, *My Life*, tr Salvator Attanasio (Weidenfeld and
Nicolson, London: 1989).
Freedman, Ralph, *Life of a Poet: Rainer Maria Rilke*, lyrical verse
tr Helen Sword with RF (Farrar Straus and Giroux, New York:
1996) [Freedman, *Life*].
Gass, William H, *Reading Rilke: Reflections on the Problems of
Translation* (Alfred Knopf, New York: 1999).
Goethe, J W, *Italian Journey 1786–1788*, tr W H Auden and
Elizabeth Mayer (Penguin Books, Harmondsworth: 1970).
Mann, Thomas, *Death in Venice and Other Stories*, tr David Luke
(Vintage, London: 1998).

Mason, Eudo C, *Rilke* (Edinburgh: 1963).

Prater, Donald A, *A Ringing Glass: the Life of Rainer Maria Rilke* (Oxford: 1994).

Ryan, Judith, *Rilke, Modernism and Poetic Tradition* (Cambridge: 1999).

Sennett, Richard, *Flesh and Stone: The Body and the City in Western Civilisation* (Faber and Faber, London and Boston: 1994).

Shakespeare, William, *The Merchant of Venice*, ed M M Mahood (Cambridge University Press, Cambridge: 1987).

von Thurn und Taxis, Marie, *Memoirs of a Princess: The Reminiscences of Princess Marie von Thurn und Taxis*, tr and compiled Nora Wydenbruck (The Hogarth Press, London: 1959) [von Thurn und Taxis, *Memoirs*].

Zweig, Stefan, *The World of Yesterday: An Autobiography* (Cassell, London: 1987; original English edition 1943; originally published in German in 1944) [Zweig, *World of Yesterday*].